YORK NOTES

WITHDRAWN

THE MERCHANT
OF VENICE

WILLIAM SHAKESPEARE

NOTES BY MICHAEL AND MARY ALEXANDER

 Longman

 York Press

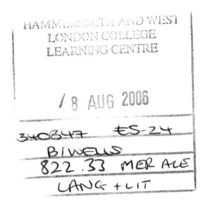
The right of Michael and Mary Alexander to be identified as the Authors
of this Work has been asserted to them in accordance with the
Copyright, Designs and Patents Act 1988

YORK PRESS
322 Old Brompton Road, London SW5 9JH

PEARSON EDUCATION LIMITED
Edinburgh Gate, Harlow,
Essex CM20 2JE, United Kingdom
Associated companies, branches and representatives throughout the world

First published 1998
This new and fully revised edition first published 2005

ISBN 1-405-80175-1

Typeset by Pantek Arts Ltd, Maidstone, Kent
Produced by Pearson Education Asia Limited, Hong Kong

CONTENTS

PART ONE

INTRODUCTION

HOW TO STUDY A PLAY

Studying on your own requires self-discipline and a carefully thought-out work plan in order to be effective.

- Drama is a special kind of writing (the technical term is 'genre') because it needs a performance in the theatre to experience a play and arrive at a full interpretation of its meaning. Try to imagine that you are a member of the audience when reading the play. Think about how it could be presented on the stage, not just about the words on the page.

- Drama is always about conflict of some sort (which may be below the surface). Identify the conflicts in the play and you will be close to identifying the large ideas or themes which bind all the parts together.

- Make careful notes on themes, character, plot and any sub-plots of the play.

- Why do you like or dislike the characters in the play? How do your feelings towards them develop and change?

- Playwrights find non-realistic ways of allowing an audience to see into the minds and motives of their characters, for example soliloquy, aside or music. Consider how such dramatic devices are used in the play you are studying.

- Think of the playwright writing the play. Why were these particular arrangements of events, characters and speeches chosen?

- Cite exact sources for all quotations, whether from the text itself or from critical commentaries. Wherever possible find your own examples from the play to back up your opinions.

- Always express your ideas in your own words.

These York Notes offer an introduction to *The Merchant of Venice* and cannot substitute for close reading of the text and the study of secondary sources.

QUESTION
What are the chief conflicts in *The Merchant of Venice*?

READING *THE MERCHANT OF VENICE*

A text of this play was first put on sale in 1600 about three years after its first performance. It has always been a popular stage play, and is said to have been performed more often than any of Shakespeare's plays except *Hamlet*. It has romance and comedy; tragedy is narrowly averted; and it offers two strong character-roles in Portia and Shylock. In the trial scene at the climax, Act IV Scene 1, the wit and skill of the heroine Portia (who is disguised as a (male) lawyer) save Antonio, the Merchant of Venice of the title, from death at the hands of Shylock the Jew. Shylock is a character who has come to dominate the theatrical history of the play.

Antonio lends his young friend Bassanio 3,000 ducats so that Bassanio can pay court to Portia, a beautiful heiress. Antonio's ships are at sea and, though a rich merchant, he has had to borrow this sum from Shylock for a term of three months. 'This fantastic bargain' gives Shylock the right to cut a pound from Antonio's flesh if the 'merry bond' (I.3.166) is not kept. All Antonio's ships fail to come to port, and his bond is forfeit. When Shylock's revenge is foiled by Portia, he is mercifully treated, but has to become a Christian.

CHECK THE BOOK
Jonathan Bate, *The Genius of Shakespeare*, 1997, is a readable general study of the playwright's work.

Shakespeare weaves the story of the flesh-bond with another story from folklore or fairytale: the beautiful heiress who by her father's will must marry the man who chooses correctly between three caskets, of gold, silver and lead. Portia, Lady of Belmont, is the heroine of both these stories. The casket scenes offer pageantry and drama, especially when Bassanio chooses the right casket.

A second romantic element is that Shylock's daughter Jessica elopes with Lorenzo, and becomes a Christian. A love scene between them introduces a last Act of moonlight and music, in which romantic confusions are magically sorted out.

But all is not sweetness and light, rescues and weddings. There are dark sides to the play, not only the threat to the life of the generous and selfless Antonio, but also in the character and situation of Shylock. He is a strongly-marked, proud, powerful character, whose emotive speeches arouse audience sympathy in spite of his merciless conduct.

So strong is the sympathy which performance can generate for Shylock that a theatrical tradition developed in the eighteenth century in which Portia's rescue of Antonio and the love of Portia and Bassanio were replaced as the chief focus by the figure of Shylock. Shylock's least attractive lines were cut out, and sometimes Act V was cut entirely. This rewriting of the play has sometimes led to the mistaken supposition that the Merchant of the title must be Shylock, a more memorable figure than the quiet Antonio.

Good plays dramatise several viewpoints, and it is unwise to be too positive about 'what Shakespeare meant' since his plays can be read in several ways. *The Merchant of Venice* reads well and makes a compelling stage play. The history of its interpretation is also interesting in itself. It reveals centuries of changing attitudes: to Christianity, to Judaism, and to religion itself; to ideals of marriage and of noble friendship; to money, merchants and usury; and to Jews. Between 1700 and 1945, audiences in England became less prejudiced against Jews, previously regarded with suspicion as Christ-killers, strange unbelievers or grasping moneylenders. The Nazi policy of exterminating Jews, brought to the attention even of those with no interest in public affairs, shocked non-Jews in English-speaking countries into reappraisal: what could have led a 'civilised' country like Germany to such a policy? Western audiences have since 1945 seen many representations, on stage and screen, in newspapers and books, of Jews as victims. This was not at all how Jews were seen by Shakespeare's Christian audience, taught that if Jews refused to accept Christ they could not as Portia puts it at IV.1.196, 'see salvation'. This teaching was supplemented by legend, hearsay and prejudice, and also by a theatrical tradition in which Jews were cruel and unreal – rather like the Nazis caricatured in post-war British films. In the medieval Mystery plays, Judas wore a red wig and a large nose; he was a comic villain, an object of ridicule. A ballad published in 1664 by Thomas Jordan, an old actor, suggests that Shakespeare's Shylock continued that tradition.

> **CONTEXT**
>
> The Bible is the key to some of this play's values. Shakespeare's contemporaries knew it from English translations such as the Geneva Bible (1560) and the Bishops' Bible (1568), which contributed to the Authorised Version of 1611.

It is now four centuries since this play first took the stage. But in the 1590s it had been three centuries since Londoners had seen a practising Jew, except perhaps in a play. For Jews had been expelled from England by King Edward I in 1290.

? QUESTION
Should we read a play four centuries old as the original audience might have done, or simply as it strikes us today?

The Merchant of Venice is a rich and successful play, full of character and incident, comedy and poetry, building up to an intensely dramatic trial and a brilliantly contrived happy ending. But the play is also a cultural document and a theatrical phenomenon whose subsequent life reveals profound changes in Western cultural attitudes between 1600 and the third millennium of the Christian era.

THE TEXT

NOTE ON THE TEXT

Shakespeare's play was first performed in 1596–8, probably in 1597. A text of *The Merchant of Venice* was printed in 1600 in quarto format, with a title page reading:

> The most excellent History [i.e., story] of the *Merchant of Venice*. With the extreame crueltie of *Shylocke* the Iewe towards the sayd Merchant, in cutting a iust [exact] pound of his fleshe: and the obtayning of *Portia* by the choyse of three chests. *As it hath beene divers times acted by the Lord Chamberlaine his servants.*

> Written by William Shakespeare.

The first performances by Shakespeare's company, the Lord Chamberlain's Men, would have been at The Theatre. The Globe did not open until 1599.

A second quarto appeared in 1619; a third text appeared in the 1623 collection of thirty-six of Shakespeare's plays in the large folio format. The 1623 volume is known as the First Folio; three further folio editions appeared in the seventeenth century. The three early texts of the play are substantially the same, fortunately, and modern texts have very few differences; one is over the character Salarino (see below). Modern editions number the lines differently, however, especially the lines of prose, for the number of words in a line depends on print size and page width. It is thought that the quarto was printed from a fair copy of Shakespeare's manuscript, and that the folio was based on the quarto, though it adds stage directions, probably from a prompt book. Act divisions were added to the plays in the First Folio; numbered scenes were added by Rowe, who edited the plays in 1714.

Most of the many trivial differences in modern texts arise from the different ways in which editors modernise Elizabethan spelling and punctuation. Some editors add further stage directions. They also standardise the names of characters prefixed to each speech. Thus

CONTEXT

A quarto was a small-format book, like a paperback, used for single plays, and cost sixpence (theatre admission cost one penny). A folio was a large-format book: the First Folio of 1623 printed 36 Shakespeare *Comedies, Histories and Tragedies* in nearly 900 double-column pages. *Folio* is Italian for leaf (of paper): one fold in folio makes 2 leaves (4 pages); two folds in quarto makes 4 leaves (8 pages).

Shylock is usually 'Iew(e)' [Jew] in quarto and folio, but modern editors regularise this to 'Shylock'.

Both quarto and folio editions have three characters, Salarino, Salerio and Solanio, but most modern editors think that Salarino disappeared into the character of Salerio in a revision of the play. Salarino is therefore found only in Mahood's (1987) and Halio's (1993) editions - two leading recent editions.

CONTEXT

The Merchant of Venice takes elements from eight known sources (see the section on Sources).

The text used for line references in these York Notes is that edited by M.M. Mahood, New Cambridge Shakespeare, Cambridge University Press, 1987, although it is not assumed that the reader has any particular edition.

For comments on other editions of *The Merchant of Venice*, see **Further reading**.

SYNOPSIS

The play combines two stories, the flesh-bond tale and the love-caskets tale. Bassanio wishes to offer marriage to Portia, the heiress of Belmont, but cannot compete with her other suitors. She is the heiress of a great fortune, but her father's will provides that she can marry only the man who chooses the casket (there are three, of gold, silver and lead) which contains her portrait.

Bassanio uses the credit of his good friend Antonio (the Merchant of Venice) to borrow 3,000 ducats from the Jewish moneylender Shylock, who hates Antonio. Antonio promises to pay the money back in three months or to allow Shylock to cut a pound of flesh from near his heart; the bond is sealed.

In Belmont, after the princes of Morocco and Arragon have chosen the wrong caskets of gold and of silver, Bassanio chooses rightly, and Portia gives him a ring which makes him her lord, and he engages never to part with it. Her gentlewoman Nerissa likewise becomes engaged to Gratiano, who wears her ring on the same terms.

All Antonio's ships are lost and his bond is forfeit. At the trial, Bassanio (who now has Portia's money) offers to repay it several times over, but Shylock wants his pound of flesh according to the bond. He sharpens his knife. The Duke hands the trial over to a young judge, Balthazar (Portia in disguise). After Shylock refuses mercy, she awards the case to him; but stipulates that no drop of blood be spilt, since that is not mentioned in the bond. Shylock asks for the money instead, but has been awarded his pound of flesh and nothing else. If he takes more or less than a pound he must die. He withdraws, but Balthazar-Portia invokes the law of Venice that no alien shall plot against the life of a citizen. The penalty is death, with confiscation of goods, half to the intended victim, half to the State.

The Duke spares Shylock's life, and will accept a fine rather than half of Shylock's goods. Antonio asks the Duke to let Shylock off all the state's half, and takes his half in trust for Shylock's daughter Jessica (who has eloped with a Christian, Lorenzo). There are two conditions: that Shylock becomes a Christian and leaves all his goods to his son-in-law and daughter. Shylock accepts. Thus Antonio leaves Shylock with half his goods and takes nothing for himself.

Bassanio offers Balthazar-Portia payment, which she declines, asking instead for the ring. Bassanio refuses, but at Antonio's suggestion sends the ring after Balthazar-Portia. Nerissa plays the same trick on Gratiano. The ladies get back to Belmont first, and ask the men for the rings which they had given them. They berate them for their infidelity, then explain the joke and forgive them. Antonio's wealth is restored, and the play ends with Portia and Bassanio, Nerissa and Gratiano, and Lorenzo and Jessica about to begin their marriages.

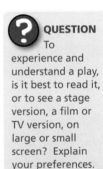

QUESTION
To experience and understand a play, is it best to read it, or to see a stage version, a film or TV version, on large or small screen? Explain your preferences.

DETAILED SUMMARIES

ACT I

SCENE 1

- Venice: Bassanio asks Antonio, the Merchant of Venice, for a loan so that he can court Portia.
- Antonio offers Bassanio his credit to borrow the money.

Antonio denies the suggestion of his younger friends that he is sad because he is worried about his ships. Alone with his 'noble kinsman' (line 57) Bassanio, Antonio asks about Bassanio's secret 'pilgrimage' (line 119). Bassanio says he has wasted the money that Antonio had advanced him; Antonio offers to help again. Embarrassed, Bassanio explains that he needs money in order to compete as a suitor with the grandees who seek the hand of Portia of Belmont, a blonde heiress of fabulous beauty and fortune. As Antonio's money is invested in ventures at sea, he offers Bassanio the use of his, Antonio's, name as credit for a loan in Venice.

COMMENTARY

The high courtesy of Venetian society derives from the wealth carried in private ships; images of great merchant ships decorate the conversation.

QUESTION
Venice's wealth is mercantile and maritime. How does this compare with London's?

Antonio is quiet, in contrast with his talkative young followers. His friend Bassanio speaks with painful elaboration until he finds that his prodigal waste of money has not affected Antonio's love.

Fortune is established as a theme: with Antonio's help, Bassanio's suit to Portia will be 'fortunate'; as Antonio's 'fortunes are at sea', he has unfortunately to rely on his credit

GLOSSARY	
6	**want-wit** fool
7	**argosies** private cargo-vessels (named after the Adriatic port of Ragusa, now Dubrovnik)

GLOSSARY

10	signors noble rulers of Venice
19	Piring looking closely
6	Andrew ship as rich as the San Andrès, captured in Cadiz in 1596 and renamed the *Andrew*
27	Vailing bowing
28	bottom hull, cargo ship
42	Janus Roman god of doorways, two-faced
50	peep through their eyes because half-closed with laughter
53	bagpiper maker of sad music
56	Nestor the wisest and oldest of the Greeks
74	respect upon regard for
84	alabaster fine stone used for figures on tombs
89	cream and mantle become opaque
89	standing stagnant
102	gudgeon a fish easily caught
110	gear matter, occasion
112	neat's tongue dried ox-tongue cured for eating vendible saleable, i.e. marriageable
123	swelling port proud deportment
125	abridged reduced
136	rate lifestyle
149–50	or ... Or either ... or
165	Brutus' Portia a noble Roman woman
169	golden fleece fleece of a golden sheep, the legendary prize ventured for by Jason and his ship the Argo on the shores (strand) of Colchis in the Black Sea
184	of my trust on my credit

CONTEXT

'Golden' is a word with legendary as well as financial significance, and this may extend to golden hair, much admired in Italy.

SCENE 2

- Belmont: Portia and Nerissa discuss Portia's father's will, by which she will marry.
- Portia reviews her suitors and favours Bassanio.

Portia is wealthy but weary: she cannot choose her husband but is to be 'chosen' by the suitor who chooses correctly between three caskets. Her gentlewoman says that the test Portia's father has

CONTEXT

The Virgin Queen, Elizabeth I, on the throne since 1558, had rejected offers of marriage from several foreign princes. In the new Europe of sovereign nation-states, national stereotyping had flourished.

devised will find a man wise enough to be worthy of her love. The six suitors who have withdrawn are caricatures of national types; Bassanio is an ideal Renaissance man; the new suitors include the dark Prince of Morocco.

COMMENTARY

Portia's weariness echoes Antonio's sadness: does wealth bring happiness? Does love?

Prose sense about love at Belmont contrasts with high-sounding poetry about money in Venice.

Some of this early scene is **exposition** (the giving of information needful to the story): we learn of the will by which Portia's father has determined her marriage.

Though accepting her father's will, Portia is hard to please – until Bassanio is mentioned.

GLOSSARY	
9	**sentences** maxims
13	**divine** theologian
16	**hot temper** ardent temperament
25–6	**who chooses his meaning** who chooses Portia's father's meaning
32	**level** take aim
33	**Neapolitan** Southern Italians were famous horsemen
37	**played false** deceived (her husband)
38	**County Palatine** Count of one of the Palatine regions of Europe (Palatine: belonging to the palace)
39–40	**And you will not have me** if you will not have me
54	**Falconbridge** a character from Shakespeare's own *King John*, a typical Englishman abroad, who speaks only his own language yet dresses in everyone else's styles
58	**come into the court** bear witness
61	**round hose** padded breeches
64	**borrowed** received
66	**sealed under for another** agreed to stand as security for another blow

---

GLOSSARY

79	Rhenish from the German Rhineland
87	Sibylla a Sybil was an ancient prophetess
	Diana goddess of chastity
108	shrive absolve in confession. Whatever his character, Portia does not want him for a husband
110	wooer rhymes with **door**

SCENE 3

- Venice: Shylock agrees to lend Bassanio 3,000 ducats, which Antonio binds himself to repay in three months, or forfeit a pound of his flesh.

Shylock hears Bassanio's request, considers whether Antonio's ships will come home; asks to speak to Antonio, but declines to eat with Christians. Shylock hates Antonio because he is a Christian, and also because he lends money gratis. He makes Antonio repeat the terms. Shylock defends usury by Jacob's example; Antonio does not accept the analogy.

COMMENTARY

Trickery is established as a theme. Shylock asks why he should lend money to one who has spat upon him. Antonio is prepared to pay a penalty. Shylock, instead of interest, proposes the bond of a pound of flesh. Antonio agrees to be bound.

QUESTION
What is usury?

Character-identification: Shylock's 'ducats' (line 1) immediately identify him as a moneylender (cf. openings of previous scenes). He is also distinguished by his speech: repetition ('monies' in lines 100–21), and alien idioms.

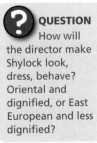

QUESTION
How will the director make Shylock look, dress, behave? Oriental and dignified, or East European and less dignified?

Shylock's 'Antonio is a *good* man' (line 11, emphasis added) assesses him as a credit risk; Bassanio takes 'good' to be an opinion on Antonio's character. Such *misunderstandings* show different assumptions and values. Shylock is first a loan-shark; then (line 26) a Jew. His religious hatred (lines 34–48) is conveyed in asides (a

CONTEXT

Jacob (line 63) Jacob *alias* Israel had twelve sons, ancestors of the twelve tribes of Israel (see **Historical background**). As son of Isaac and grandson of **Abra(ha)m** (line 64), Jacob was the **third possessor** (line 66) of the birthright of Abraham, but only through the work of **his wise mother** line (65), Rebecca, who helped him trick the blind old Isaac into granting it to Jacob rather than to his elder (twin) brother Esau. To flee Esau's rage Jacob served his uncle **Laban** (line 69) for seven years in order to win his daughter Rachel; but Laban tricked him into marrying his eldest daughter Leah. Jacob paid Laban back by getting him to agree that he could keep any sheep and goats born spotted; Jacob then increased their number by a trick of his own. God could reward cunning – in a Patriarch.

theatre convention: words spoken to the audience, inaudible to those on the stage, as in lines 33 and 48) to show his secretiveness. He then displays his feelings, provoking Antonio; shows him 'kindness', revealing only later the 'merry bond' which gives him his chance of revenge.

GLOSSARY

1	**ducats** gold coins (so called after the Duke or Doge of Venice)
4	**For the which ... bound** committed in writing
6	**stead** help
	pleasure oblige
14	**sufficient** financially acceptable as security
15	**in supposition** presumed
	Tripolis Lebanese port
16	**the Indies** India
	Rialto the business centre of Venice (*not* the Rialto Bridge)
26	**assured ... assured** reassured ... financially secured
28	**the Nazarite** Jesus of Nazareth, who expelled the demons possessing two men; the demons rushed into a herd of pigs (Matthew 8:28). Jews are forbidden by religious law to eat pork; and regard Jesus as no more than a prophet
33	**fawning publican** in the Gospels, publicans are Jewish tax-collectors for the Romans and therefore traitors. Jesus included publicans among his friends. Antonio is 'fawning' because he comes to beg of Shylock. But Christ tells a parable favourably contrasting the humility before God of a publican with the arrogance of a Pharisee (Luke 18:9–14). The phrase has different implications for Jews and for Christians
37	**usance** euphemism for usury (cf. lines 42–3)
38	**upon the hip** (wrestling term) at a disadvantage
42	**thrift** (euphemism for interest) thriving
43	**my tribe** the Jewish people as a whole not one of its twelve tribes
45	**store** wealth
47	**gross** full sum
50	**But soft** Wait!
51	**in our mouths** we were speaking of
62	**Upon advantage** To your own profit
62	**use** practise (with perhaps a dig at 'usance' (line 37 above))

GLOSSARY

70	**compromised** agreed
71	**eanlings** new-born lambs
72	**rank** in heat, ready for sexual intercourse
74	**work of generation** breeding
76	**pilled me** peeled; **me** a colloquial 'ethical dative' adding nothing to the sense
	wands sticks
77	**deed of kind** mating
78	**fulsome** pregnant (it was believed that offspring resembled what the mother was looking at when she conceived)
79	**eaning** bearing
80	**Fall** produce
83	**venture** risk (Antonio distinguishes between his venture capitalism involving effort, risk and providence, and Shylock's usury – see section on **Usury**)
86	**inserted** brought in (by Shylock)
87	**Or is your gold … rams?** a rhetorical question expecting the answer no, for money does not multiply by nature
89	**note me** listen (Antonio has turned aside)
99	**rated** berated
101	**Still have I** I have always
104	**gaberdine** loose cloak
109	**void your rheum** spit
126	**A breed … metal** a profit from increase of metal, which does not reproduce in the way of living creatures
127	**break** become bankrupt
133	**doit** a small Dutch coin of little value
134	**kind** natural kindness
135	**This were kindness** This would indeed be kindness
138	**single** simple, unconditional
	merry sport joke
142	**nominated** named
	equal exact
145	**seal** give my seal (impress it in wax)
168	**fearful** untrustworthy
170	**gentle** (pun) kind / Gentile, repeated throughout the play

CHECK THE BOOK

The Bible is the book Shakespeare's audience knew best. *The Merchant* contrasts the values of the first books of the Old Testament with those of the New Testament. Read the stories the play refers to, e.g., the parable of the Prodigal Son, in the Authorised Version.

ACT II

SCENE 1

- Belmont: Morocco learns the terms of the task.

Portia says she is not put off by Morocco's dark skin. The proud Prince agrees never to marry if he should choose the wrong casket.

COMMENTARY

Exoticism is a theme of the play. Venice (see **Historical background**) is exotic and Belmont is more so. The Prince's words emphasise his darkness, prowess and pride. Dress would show Morocco as the most exotic of the suitors. (Venice employed Moors as soldiers to defend her Mediterranean empire; Shakespeare's *Othello* is subtitled *The Moor of Venice*. Moors had the glamour of an enemy who is no longer dangerous, unlike the Turks.)

CHECK THE BOOK

C. L. Barber *Shakespeare's Festive Comedy*, 1972 is still a good scholarly and critical introduction to the genre.

GLOSSARY	
	flourish short call
	cornets woodwind horns
	tawny light-skinned (unlike a 'blackamoor')
2	livery distinctive clothing
3	near bred brought up
5	Phoebus' fire heat of the (god of the) sun
6	incision cut
9	feared frightened
14	nice fastidious
17	scanted restricted
25	Sophy the Shah of Persia
26	Solyman Suleiman the Magnificent, Sultan of Turkey
30	a roars he roars
32	Lichas servant who brought Hercules a poisoned shirt, and was thrown into the sea in his rage
35	Alcides a Greek name of Hercules
43	be advised think it over

SCENE 2

- Venice: We are introduced to Lancelot Gobbo and his father.

The clown Lancelot Gobbo resolves to leave Shylock's service. He fools about with his blind old father. Bassanio agrees to take on Lancelot as a servant. He orders a feast for the evening. Graziano promises to be quiet if he is allowed to accompany Bassanio to Belmont.

COMMENTARY

Lancelot, the Clown or professional comedian, makes out that he is torn between 'conscience' (line 1) and 'the fiend' (Devil) (line 8), like a character in an old Morality Play. He is modelled on the Vice, a comic attendant on the Devil in those plays. His comic patter is full of meaningless phrases, repetition, confusion and malapropism (using the wrong word). His role is to make the audience laugh, although not everything in his patter is nonsense. In Italian *gobbo* means 'hunchback', a figure of Venetian folklore.

> **QUESTION**
> What is the function of the comic scenes in the play?

GLOSSARY		
8	pack	go
	Fia! away! (Italian *via*)	
10	neck of my heart anatomically absurd phrase	
13	smack … taste sexually suggestive words	
18	God … mark! routine apology before something indelicate (cf. modern 'Pardon my French'), like 'saving your reverence' (lines 19–20)	
21	incarnation (malapropism) incarnate	
27	true-begotten (malapropism) true begetter	
28	sand-blind nearly blind	
	high gravel-blind more nearly blind (a Gobbo-ism)	
29	confusions (malapropism) conclusions; to 'try conclusions' was to try or prove an experiment or to propose riddles	
35	Be God's sonties by God's saints	
39	the waters a storm (of tears)	
40	'master' the title of one who has (rather than is) a servant	

CONTEXT

For a son to make a fool of his father reverses Elizabethan and Jewish norms. But Gobbo does so, and Jacob had done so.

GLOSSARY

41–2	well to live in good health
46	*ergo* therefore (Latin, used by the learned)
51	sisters three the classical Fates
54	staff of my age biblical phrase
56	hovel-post prop for a shelter
57	father old man
63	a wise father Gobbo reverses the old proverb
64	[*Kneels*] traditional stage business (physical actions accompanying the words) is for the son to kneel facing the wrong way so that at line 77 old Gobbo feels his son's hair instead of his chin
64–5	Give me your blessing Jacob's request to Isaac, prompted by his 'wise mother' (I.3.65)
77	thou a change from the respectful 'you'
78	fill-horse draught-horse
84	set up my rest bet my bottom dollar
86	very Jew a real miser
	halter hangman's noose
87–8	tell every … ribs reversing the usual saying
91	a Jew which I am not (cf. 'I'm a Dutchman')
99	Gramercy from French '(May God) grant (you) mercy'
103	infection (malapropism) affection, desire
107	cater-cousins cousins who entertain each other
110	frutify (malapropism?) notify
111	dish of doves a humble countryman's present
113	impertinent (malapropism) pertinent
118	defect (malapropism) effect, upshot
121	preferred recommended
124	old proverb 'The grace of God is enough'
	parted divided
130	guarded ornamented (perhaps as a Fool)
131	I cannot get Lancelot is boasting that he *can*
133	table palm (placed on a Bible)
135	small trifle (irony) fortune-telling by palm-reading indicates Lancelot's prodigious luck in marriage (cf. that of his new master)

GLOSSARY	
136	coming-in only a beginning
138	featherbed i.e., marriage is more dangerous than a voyage at sea
	scapes adventures
139	gear occasion
140	twinkling of an eye: a moment
152	rude outspoken
156	liberal easy-going
159	misconstered misconstrued
167	sad ostent grave outward show

CHECK THE BOOK

Russ McDonald, *Shakespeare and the Arts of Language*, 2001, discusses Shakespeare's use of verse and prose in a range of plays.

SCENE 3

- Venice: Jessica sends a letter to Lorenzo.

Jessica gives Lancelot a letter for Lorenzo, with whom she will elope and become a Christian.

COMMENTARY

The last piece setting up the plot is introduced rapidly and simply, though attention is drawn to Jessica's lack of filial feeling. The final couplet (pair of rhyming lines) gives a clear signal to the future.

GLOSSARY	
10	exhibit (malapropism) inhibit

SCENE 4

- Venice: Lorenzo teels Gratiano of his plan of elopement.

Lorenzo receives Jessica's letter and bids Lancelot tell Jessica that he will not fail her. Lorenzo tells Gratiano of the plan of elopement: Jessica will be disguised as a boy torchbearer at the supper.

CONTEXT

Females were played by boys on Elizabethan stages, so acting was not realistic. Disguise is a device of comedy. In romantic comedy, girls can disguise as boys, as Jessica does here, and as Portia does later.

COMMENTARY

This scene runs on from the last. It repeats the Christian justification for Jessica's elopement

GLOSSARY

2	**Disguise** for the masque at supper
6	**quaintly** skilfully
10	**break up** unseal
12	**the hand** the handwriting
15	**By your leave** excuse me
36	**Unless she do it** unless misfortune does it
37	**That she is** that Jessica is
38	**faithless** without Christian faith

SCENE 5

- Venice: Shylock asks Jessica to lock up.

As he leaves the house for supper, Shylock bids his daughter lock up while he is out, especially when he hears that there will be a masque at Bassanio's supper. Lancelot gives her Lorenzo's message.

COMMENTARY

Contrast Shylock's miserliness towards his former servant with his own willingness to grow fat at the expense of Christian wasters. Shylock is made to forget that he will not eat with Christians (I.3.30); has Shakespeare forgotten, or has Shylock changed his mind?

There is much made of the supper and the masque, but this seems to serve chiefly to divert Shylock's attention. Although Shylock's attendance allows Jessica to escape, he could have been made to sleep through it. Does the elaborate locking-up serve a dramatic purpose?

GLOSSARY

3	**What, Jessica!** a sharp summons, repeated
5	**rend apparel out** rip clothing; perhaps letting it out because Lancelot was getting fat?

8	could do … bidding (pun) would do nothing without being called / would accomplish nothing without calling (others)
16	Look to guard
17	rest (pun) peace / hoard
18	dream of money bags i.e., that he would lose money, since dreams were supposed to go by opposites
	tonight last night
20	reproach for 'approach'? ('reproach' also fits)
22	conspired Lancelot is indiscreet
24	Black Monday Easter Monday. Nose-bleeds were bad luck; a rigmarole mocking Shylock's dream-lore
32	varnished (pun) masked / drunken
35	Jacob's staff Jacob left for Laban's with only a staff and returned a rich man; an example of 'thrift'
41	worth a Jewès eye worth a Jew's inspection, hence a rich gem
42	that … Hagar's offspring a line full of tribal resentment. To Shylock, Christians are outcasts, having left the house of Israel; and thus are sons of Hagar. Hagar, Abraham's concubine, fled his house complaining of harsh treatment (cf. Lancelot and Jessica). Hagar's son was Ishmael, a mocker, like Lancelot
44	patch fool

QUESTION The bargains of the flesh-bond and the casket-choosing are highly improbable. Does this matter?

Scene 6

- Venice: Jessica elopes with Lorenzo.

Lorenzo joins his masked friends by Shylock's house; Jessica throws him a casket and joins him, dressed as a boy. Antonio says Bassanio's ship is ready to depart.

Commentary

Gratiano's memorable comment on young love is given prominence just before we see the elopement. Why?

Why does Shakespeare have Jessica throw Lorenzo a casket, and why does she further 'gild' herself?

Scene 6 continued

CHECK THE BOOK

Carol Rumens,ed., *Clamorous Voices: Shakespeare's Women Today*, 1987, examines the roles of women in a range of plays, from a modern feminist viewpoint.

GLOSSARY	
1	**penthouse** shelter with sloping roof
5	**the clock** the time of their meeting
6	**pigeons** doves drawing the chariot of Venus
9	**unforfeited** unbroken (newly betrothed lovers are keener than faithful spouses to keep their word)
15	**younger** the Prodigal was a **younger** son (Luke 15:11–32). Some editors prefer the spelling younker, a young nobleman
16	**scarfèd bark** beflagged ship (of love)
17	**strumpet** prostitute (cf. the harlots with whom the Prodigal wastes his substance, inviting but false)
19	**overweathered ribs** worn timbers
22	**abode** stay
26	**my father Jew** my Jewish father-in-law
34	**catch this casket** (cf. the catching of Portia via a casket)
36	**exchange** change of role: girl-boy/daughter-wife
44	**office of discovery** job which is to uncover
46	**lovely garnish** lovely outward trappings
50	**gild** cover thinly with gold
51	**moe** a greater number of
52	**gentle** (pun) generous / gentile
59	**gentleman** i.e., Jessica
65	**No masque ... come about** a switch of plan

SCENE 7

- Belmont: Morocco fails to choose the correct casket.

Morocco chooses the golden casket, proud to gain 'what many men desire' (line 5). Inside is a skull.

COMMENTARY

The scene both opens and closes with stage directions, from Portia: 'draw aside the curtains' (line 1) and 'Draw the curtain' (line 78) – the curtains hide the caskets, which in turn hide the fate of her suitors.

Proud Morocco goes for gold and finds death. Does this bear on the play's themes?

GLOSSARY

1	**discover** uncover
2	**several** different
8	**all as blunt** quite as unappealing (as lead)
9	**hazard** venture
12	**withal** too
22	**virgin hue** colour of the moon/Diana/chastity
25	**an even hand** impartially
26	**estimation** repute
40	**mortal breathing** living (unlike the saint in a shrine)
41	**Hyrcanian** south of the Caspian sea
51	**To rib ... cerecloth** enclose (in lead) her waxed shroud
53	**tried** assayed, purified
56	**angel** the archangel St Michael
57	**insculped upon** engraved on top of
63	**A carrion death** dead figure of Death: skull
72	**inscrolled** written on this scroll
73	**suit is cold** proverb announcing failure
75	**welcome frost** hello to single life
78	**A gentle riddance!** a pleasing departure

CHECK THE BOOK
Shakespeare has a vocabulary of 30,000 words, hundreds of which appear for the first time in his writing. David Crystal, *Shakespeare's Words*, 2002, is a clear and expert guide.

SCENE 8

- Venice: Bassanio has sailed.

Shylock raises the alarm: daughter and ducats are gone, he suspects with Bassanio. We hear that one of Antonio's ships is lost, and of his grief at parting with Bassanio.

COMMENTARY

This is a scene of **exposition** reported in conversation.

It is made clear Jessica was not in Bassanio's ship; Antonio and Bassanio play no part in her abduction.

Antonio's feelings at losing first a ship and then Bassanio are to be compared with Shylock's reaction to the loss of his ducats and his daughter.

What conclusions should we draw?

It is now clear that Antonio loves Bassanio.

CONTEXT

A 'ducat' bore the image of the Duke, or Doge, of Venice. The honour of Venice is involved in the justice of its legal and financial transactions.

GLOSSARY

7	given to understand led to believe
15	daughter the 'ght' may have been pronounced
16	Christian ducats won from Christians and now lost to them
19	double ducats two-ducat coins
24	his stones (pun) jewels / testicles
25	keep his day pay up on the appointed day
28	reasoned talked
40	Slubber perform in a slovenly way
41	stay ... riping wait for the ripest moment
43	mind of love thoughts when contemplating love
45	ostents demonstrations
46	conveniently appropriately
49	affection ... sensible emotion strangely evident
51	he only loves ... him i.e., Bassanio is all he lives for
54	quicken ... heaviness lighten the grief he hugs to him

SCENE 9

- Belmont: Arragon fails too.

Arragon chooses the silver casket to 'get as much as he deserves' (line 35). Inside is a fool's head. News of the arrival of Bassanio excites Portia.

COMMENTARY

Arragon has the arrogance suggested by his name. He is Prince of Aragon, part of Spain, which was the great power of Europe, ruler of southern Italy and enemy to England.

He chooses not what many men desire but what he believes he deserves: 'I will assume desert' (line 50). He scorns the fool multitude and gets a fool's head.

Portia's readiness to love Bassanio is again made very clear.

CHECK THE BOOK

The English poet W.H. Auden's essay 'Brothers and Others' (in *The Dyer's Hand*, 1963), offers an interesting perspective on Antonio as a perhaps homosexual outsider.

GLOSSARY		
	Servitor	servant
1	straight	immediately
2	election	choice
18	addressed me	prepared myself
24–5	be meant By	refer to
26	fond	foolish
27	martlet	house-martin
29	force … casualty	power and path of accident
31	jump with	join
37	cozen	deceive
41	derived	obtained
42	clear honour	noble honour
43	cover	keep their hats on
45	gleaned	discarded (from harvested corn)
48	new varnished	dusted and made bright again
54	schedule	scroll
60	judge	to judge
61	offices	roles
65	shadows	phantoms, likenesses
67	iwis	for sure
68	Silvered o'er	covered in silver (decorations worn by court officials)
69	Take what wife	'Perhaps the poet had forgotten that he who missed Portia was never to marry any woman' (Dr Johnson)
70	head	you will always be like me (a fool)
72	sped	dealt with
77	wroth	wrath, anger
79	deliberate	deliberating
80	They have … to lose	they have enough intelligence to choose wrongly
84	my lord	you, sir (a little joke)

GLOSSARY	
86	**Venetian** i.e., Gratiano
88	**sensible regreets** tangible greetings (see line 90)
93	**costly** gorgeous
94	**forespurrer** one who rides before
97	**highday** feast day, celebratory
99	**post** messenger
100	**Bassanio ... will it be!** O Cupid, let it be Bassanio!

ACT III

SCENE 1

- Venice: Shylock resolves to have revenge.

Antonio's friends lament the loss of his ship, laugh at Shylock's loss of his daughter. Tubal reports that Jessica is squandering Shylock's money; and that another of Antonio's ships is lost. Shylock resolves to 'have the heart' (line 100) of Antonio.

COMMENTARY

More exposition by Antonio's talkative friends.

Losses are balanced: Shylock's daughter, Antonio's ship.

Shylock's 'Let him look to his bond', thrice repeated (lines 37,38 and 39), warns that his motive (despite his speech on the common humanity of Jew and Christian) is revenge.

Cruel Gentile mockery should not conceal the fact that the father does indeed seem to miss ducats more than his only daughter.

The effect of Tubal's alternation of bad and good news is to torture Shylock. Tubal's news confirms Shylock's desire to torture Antonio.

Is Tubal unmotivated, comic?

GLOSSARY

2	**unchecked** uncontradicted
3	**Goodwins** the Goodwin Sands at the mouth of the Thames
7	**knapped** munched
9	**slips** counterfeits
10	**crossing** deviating from
13	**full stop** conclusion
17	**betimes** quickly
17	**cross** spoil
23	**wings** i.e., the clothes of a page
24	**fledged** fit to fly
25	**complexion** disposition
29	**old carrion** you old corpse
	Rebels it does it rebel (in having a 'disobedient' erection)? (Solanio pretends to misunderstand)
33	**Rhenish** a fine (white) wine from the Rhine
35	**match** bargain, deal
37	**look to** keep
40	**forfeit** fail, incur the penalty
42	**bait** use as bait for
47	**dimensions** parts
	affections reactions
54	**what is his humility?** what form does his humility take?
55	**what ... sufferance** what form should his forbearance take
56–7	**it shall go hard but** assuredly
61	**matched** found equal
67	**curse** Christ's prophecy of the destruction of Jerusalem
71	**hearsed** laid out
	No news of them i.e., of the jewels
93–4	**for a monkey** to buy a monkey
96	**of Leah** from Leah (his wife)
99	**fee me** hire for me
102	**synagogue** perhaps to swear the oath of IV.1.225

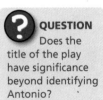

QUESTION
Does the title of the play have significance beyond identifying Antonio?

CONTEXT

Stage properties, known as 'props' such as caskets and rings, or Shylock's knife and scales, can act as powerful visual symbols on stage.

SCENE 2

- Belmont: Bassanio's joy and grief.

Portia is anxious, but Bassanio chooses the lead casket containing Portia's portrait. They rejoice; she gives him a ring which he must keep. Gratiano and Nerissa also become engaged. Lorenzo brings a letter from Antonio: his ships are lost, his bond is forfeit. Bassanio goes to him.

COMMENTARY

Portia is seriously in love, yet her second speech (lines 40–62) is fanciful and **mock-heroic** (using heroic comparisons, e.g., 'Go, Hercules', for playful purposes).

Apart from initial *flourishes* on the cornets, the song 'Tell me where is fancy bred' (line 63) is the first music in the play. Its connection of music with love is developed in Act V.

The engagement of Portia and Bassanio is golden; Gratiano's engagement repeats the tune in a lower, brassier key.

The bad news changes the notes to tragic, but Bassanio still speaks of engagements (lines 260–1).

GLOSSARY	
6	**quality** manner
14	**Beshrew** a mild curse
15	**if mine then yours** because husband and wife are one flesh
18	**these naughty times** this worthless age
22	**peize** weigh down, slow down
23	**eche** eke out
24	**election** choosing
25	**rack** i.e., of time. Instrument of torture on which traitors were stretched to make them confess
29	**fear** fear for
33	**enforcèd** under torture
42	**aloof** apart

GLOSSARY

44	swan-like it was believed that the mute swan sang before dying
49	flourish fanfare
54	presence dignity
55	Alcides Hercules, who rescued a beautiful virgin from the sea-monster. As reward, he asked for Laomedon's famous horses rather than the girl (hence 'with much more love'). A tale from Ovid's *Metamorphoses*
56	howling weeping
57	stand for sacrifice am ready to die
58	Dardanian wives Trojan women
59	blearèd tear-stained
61	Live thou should you live
69	fancy fantasy, sexual attraction
	cradle in its infancy in the eye
73	So may ... themselves may outward appearances fade away (Bassanio's thoughts as he looks at the caskets echo those of the song)
74	still ever
84	stayers ropes
86	livers white as milk a bloodless liver was a sign of cowardice. (Antonio's pound of flesh has to be bloodless.)
87	excrement growth, i.e., a beard
88	redoubted feared
89	purchased ... weight (cosmetics) bought by the ounce
91	lightest most fickle and faithless
95	supposèd what is thought
	dowry ... head legacy of another's head
97	guilèd treacherous
99	Indian dusky (not fair, not beautiful)
102	Hard ... Midas everything Midas touched turned to gold, including his food. From the *Metamorphoses* of Ovid
103	drudge slave (silver; common coinage)
104	meagre poor
106	paleness lack of colour
109	As such as
112	scant ration
115	counterfeit picture

CONTEXT

Belmont, an estate on the mainland, is the less realistic 'other place' often found in a Shakespeare play.

GLOSSARY

122	**golden mesh** a hair-net of gold wire
124	**How could he see** (when blinded by her eyes)
130	**continent** that which contains
132	**Chance as fair** hazard as fortunately
140	**by note** as instructed
157	**Exceed account** love's blessings are uncountable
174	**vantage to exclaim on** opportunity to accuse
191	**none from me** none to be unavailable to me (i.e., for there is plenty of joy to go round)
195	**so thou canst get** as long as you can get
199	**intermission** idle time
202	**sweat** sweated
203	**roof** i.e., of the mouth
213	**play** wager
215–16	**stake down ... stake down** put down the money now ... with a limp penis
220	**youth** recentness
	interest influence
222	**very friends** true friends
226	**My purpose ... here** it was not my purpose to have seen you here
231	**Commends ... you** sends you his greetings
235	**estate** age, condition
236	**stranger** newcomer, i.e., Jessica
238	**royal** superlative
240	**Jasons** see I.1.169
	fleece (pun) fleets
242	**shrewd** painful
254	**Ran in my veins** was my (gentle) blood
260	**engaged** pledged
261	**mere** absolute
266	**hit** succeeded
268	**Barbary** North Africa (land of the Berbers)
271	**should appear** seems
275	**confound** destroy
277	**impeach** discredit
	freedom legal protection

CHECK THE BOOK
On how the words should be spoken, see Cicely Berry, *The Actor and His Text*, 1987, and Patsy Rodenburg, *Speaking Shakespeare*, 2002.

GLOSSARY

281	envious malicious
298	deface cancel
18	use your pleasure follow your inclination

SCENE 3

- Venice: Antonio expects death.

Shylock refuses to listen to Antonio: he is determined to have his bond, relying on the strict law of Venice. Antonio hopes Bassanio will come before he dies.

COMMENTARY

The scene makes evident the intensity of Shylock's vengefulness and establishes Antonio's patient resignation.

GLOSSARY

9	naughty worthless
19	kept dwelt
20	bootless unprofitable
22	forfeitures penalties for breach of contract
24	Therefore That is why
27	commodity access to our privileges
31	Consisteth of relies upon the equal standing of
32	so bated me made me so thin

SCENE 4

- Belmont: Portia follows Bassanio.

Portia leaves her estate in the hands of Lorenzo and Jessica, while she withdraws to a convent. She sends a messenger to her cousin Dr Bellario in Padua, and tells Nerissa that they are to adopt male disguise.

CHECK THE NET
The Shakespeare Birthplace Trust website is an excellent general resource on all aspects of Shakespeare's life, search http://shakespeare.org.uk

COMMENTARY

Lorenzo establishes the Renaissance idea of noble male friendship as 'god-like' (line 3). Portia's acceptance of this ideal prompts her generosity throughout the play.

The women's disguise as men, and the fiction of the convent, are conventions of romantic comedy.

GLOSSARY	
2	conceit conception
3	amity (Platonic) friendship (see **Themes on love, marriage and friendship**)
9	Than customary … you than your usual generosity can make you
12	waste spend
15	lineaments characteristics
17	bosom lover intimate friend and confidant
20	In purchasing … soul in redeeming my soul's image, i.e., Bassanio's friend
21	state of hellish cruelty hell of victimhood
25	husbandry and manage care and management
33	imposition charge
52	imagined speed the speed of imagination
53	traject ferry (Italian *traghetto*)
62	that we lack i.e., masculine characteristics
68	'frays affrays, fights
69	quaint elaborate
72	do withal help it
77	raw immature
	jacks knaves
78	turn to turn into (not, as Portia pretends, 'turn towards', though this must be in the minds of newly-weds whose wedding night has been postponed)
80	If thou … interpreter if overheard by someone who thought it indecent
81	device plan

SCENE 5

• Belmont: Jessica and Lorenzo praise Portia.

Jessica is now a Christian; she and her husband praise Portia and
Lord Bassanio.

COMMENTARY

Lancelot's fooling should not conceal the serious contention that
stealing her away is justified by the salvation of her soul.

Lorenzo again extols Portia's nobility, and although he and Jessica
end jokingly, many a true word is spoken in jest in this play.

GLOSSARY

1	**the sins of the father** quoted from the second verse of the first of the Ten Commandments given to Moses; referring to Shylock	
2	**fear you** fear for you	
3	**agitation** for 'cogitation'?	
6	**bastard** ill-founded	
	neither anyway	
8	**got** begot	
10–11	**sins of my mother** i.e., of adultery, in conceiving Jessica outside wedlock	
15	**I shall be saved by my husband** 'The unbelieving wife is sanctified by the husband' (I Corinthians 7:14)	
16	**enow** enough (an economic joke: if pork-eaters outnumber pigs, bacon prices will rise)	
19	**a rasher** bacon	
25	**are out** i.e., of corners and of sympathy	
30	**commonwealth** society	
31	**Moor** a black attendant on Morocco?	
33	**more than reason** bigger than reasonable	
34	**less than ... honest** unchaste	
	more (pun) better	
38	**sirrah** sir (used in rebuke to a servant)	
40	**stomachs** appetites	
43	**'cover'** lay the table	

CONTEXT

Scylla ... Charybdis (line 13) In Homer's *Odyssey*, Ulysses had to steer between the monster Scylla and the whirlpool of Charybdis in the straits between Italy and Sicily. This reference to a noble adventure is turned by Lancelot into a joke against Shylock/Scylla (similar in sound) and Jessica's mother, whom he could 'fall into'.

GLOSSARY

45	**duty** i.e., not to cover (my head with a hat)
46	**occasion** opportunity to make a pun
52	**humours and conceits** inclinations and fancies
53	**O dear discretion** What fine discrimination!
57	**Garnished** equipped
58	**Defy the matter** avoid the point
68	**lay** bet
70	**Pawned** added as a stake
78	**set you forth** praise you

ACT IV

SCENE 1

- Venice: the trial scene.
- Shylock insists on his bond. Portia (disguised as an advocate) is made judge in the case.
- Shylock refuses mercy and insists on justice according to his bond. She awards him the penalty – but he must not take a drop of blood, or more or less than a pound of flesh, on penalty of death. Shylock is foiled.
- Portia invokes another law by which an alien who has tried to kill a Venetian must lose his life and his property.
- Shylock is let off both penalties, on conditions: that he become a Christian; and leave his money to Lorenzo and Jessica.
- The only payment Portia will accept from Bassanio is his ring.

CONTEXT

The University of Padua, the nearest large city to Venice, and part of Venice's possessions on the mainland, had a famous faculty of Civil Law.

Antonio patiently awaits his fate. Shylock refuses the Duke's plea for clemency and Bassanio's offer of twice the money, and whets his knife. Nerissa, dressed as a lawyer's clerk, brings a letter from the lawyer Bellario to the Duke, commending a young doctor Balthasar (Portia in disguise) to try the case.

Portia commends mercy to Shylock, who demands justice. She gives judgment in his favour, according to the bond, and Antonio bids farewell to Bassanio. Portia warns Shylock not to take a drop of blood, which is not in the bond. He now tries to take Bassanio's earlier offer but this is disallowed; he is due exactly one pound of flesh. He asks for the 3,000 ducats, but can have his bond only. He tries to leave, but Portia accuses him as an alien of seeking the life of a Venetian. The penalty is to pay half his goods to the Venetian, the other half to the State, while his life is in forfeit to the Duke.

The Duke grants him his life and offers to mitigate the State's share. Antonio asks the Duke to waive the State's share, and says he will hold his half-share in trust for Lorenzo and Jessica, provided Shylock becomes a Christian and leaves his estate to Lorenzo and Jessica. Shylock accepts.

QUESTION
What is the function of Gratiano in this scene?

Balthazar-Portia has to leave urgently. She refuses Bassanio's offer of payment but asks for his ring. He refuses, but when urged by Antonio sends it after her.

COMMENTARY

The content of this scene is discussed in **Extended commentaries, text 2**.

The following comments relate to its dramatic structure.

Shylock's answer to why he wants his pound of flesh (lines 35–62) is insulting; it also shows how far he is in the grip of hatred.

He stands on his rights, making an analogy with the legal rights of Christian slave-holders (lines 89–103) which exposes Christian hypocrisy.

Shylock's knife and scales add symbolic meaning as well as drama. He believes in law and sacrifice.

Portia speaks for mercy, but denies Bassanio's plea that the law be relaxed, since the letter of the law offers her her only opportunity.

The Duke and Antonio show mercy and magnanimity to a defeated foe, in contrast to Gratiano's insults.

The moral blackmail used by Portia to get her ring back succeeds because of Antonio's sense of obligation.

Scene 1 continued

GLOSSARY	
	Magnificoes judges elected by the nobility
7	qualify moderate
10	envy malice
18	but lead'st ... fashion only maintain this pretence
19	last hour of act last moment before performance
20	remorse more strange more wonderful pity
24	loose surrender
26	moiety half
32	Turks ... Tartars who do not share the religious traditions which Jews have in common with Christians
35	possessed informed
36	sworn presumably in the synagogue at the end of Act III Scene 1
39	charter a mistake: Venice did not have a charter from the Crown, as an English city would
43	humour predisposition resulting from the balance of bodily fluids; cf. the loose modern use of 'allergy'
46	baned poisoned
50	affection physical reaction
60	lodged fixed
62	losing (for he would lose 3,000 ducats)
70	think remember
72	main flood bate high tide decrease
88	How shalt ... mercy cf. James 2:13 'For there shall be judgement merciless to him that showeth no mercy'
90	many a purchased slave i.e., in Venice. But Shylock has a general point: slavery was practised throughout Christian Europe including England
103	I stand for judgement cf. IV.1.142 and Portia at III.2.57 and Antonio at IV.1
104	Upon by
106	determine settle
113	one drop of blood (an unremarked prophecy)
115	tainted wether a diseased castrated ram. Abraham substituted a ram provided by God for Isaac (Genesis 22:13)
121	whet sharpen
128	inexecrable beyond cursing

CONTEXT

In 'whet' (line 121) and 'sole' (line 123) Shakespeare tells us that Shylock here sharpens his knife on his shoe. Is Antonio, ' a tainted wether' (line 115), to be the sacrifice?

GLOSSARY

130	**faith** Christian belief, incompatible with the teachings of Pythagoras
131	**To hold opinion with** to agree
	Pythagoras early Greek philosopher who believed in the transmigration of souls
134	**hanged** (predatory animals could be tried and executed until the late seventeenth century)
135	**fell** cruel
	fleet flit
136	**unhallowed dam** unholy mother
138	**starved** deadly
139	**rail** declaim abusively
140	**but offend'st** only does harm
151–2	**in loving visitation** on a friendly visit
153	**Balthazar** Portia has adopted the name of her servant at III.4.45, whom she sent to her cousin Dr Bellario to collect 'notes and garments'. By a dramatic coincidence, the Duke too consults Bellario of Padua; but the Duke is not aware of Portia's plot
159	**let him lack** deprive him of
161–2	**whose trial … commendation** the test you make of him will recommend him better than my words
170	**Which is the merchant …?** this question is standard court procedure. The judge requires the principals to identify themselves
175	**impugn** disallow
176	**danger** power
180	**The quality … strained** the nature of mercy is such that it is not constrained or compelled
182	**It blesseth** cf. Acts 20:35 'It is more blessed to give than to receive'
195–6	**none of us Should see salvation** cf. Psalm 102:10–11, part of morning prayer: 'He hath not dealt with us after our sins, nor rewarded us according to our iniquities. For as high as the heaven is above the earth, so great is his mercy toward them that fear him'
197	**that same prayer** the Lord's Prayer ('Forgive us our trespasses, as we forgive them that trespass against us')
199	**mitigate** make more gentle
202	**My deeds … head!** cf. Matthew 27:25

? QUESTION
How would you produce the outcome of the trial and Shylock's exit? Some Victorian productions stopped the play here. The actor-director Sir Henry Irving, left alone on stage, knocked twice on the door of his empty house. Long silence. Final curtain.

CONTEXT

Daniel (line 219) – Shylock compares Portia to Daniel, the young judge who in the biblical story of Susannah and the Elders (Daniel 13) detects the fraud of the elders and prevents injustice. In the Bible Daniel is also called Baltassar

GLOSSARY

210	bears down overthrows
241–5	power in Venice ... establishèd Venice's respect for her own laws was legendary
217	precedent the chief rule of English common law
223	thrice Portia increases this from Bassanio's 'twice'; but in line 208 he less clearly offers 'ten times'
224	oath presumably in the synagogue in Act III Scene 1
231	tenour wording
238	stay take my stand
243	Hath full relation fully authorises
251	balance a plural, and doubly symbolic: the scales of Justice to weigh impartially the merits of a case; Shylock's scales for weighing one pound.
260	armed fortified in mind
264	still ever
274	Repent but you regret only
277	with all my heart willingly. To make a jest on the point of death shows the Renaissance gentleman's ability to make light of things, known as *sprezzatura*
292	Barabbas (stressed on the first syllable) the name of the thief whom the Jewish mob released instead of Jesus; the name also of Marlowe's Jew of Malta; and of a thief in Shakespeare's *Measure for Measure*
316	Soft wait
326	scruple an apothecary's weight; one-twentieth of a scruple is one grain
335	merely purely
342	I'll stay ... question I'll remain no longer to argue the case. Shylock tries to leave
350	privy coffer personal treasury
352	'gainst all other voice without appeal
359	Down Kneel
364	our royal plural; also a Christian
368	Which humbleness ... which asking pardon will reduce to a fine
377	quit remit
379	in use to administer in trust

GLOSSARY

382	**Two things … more**	with two further conditions
383	**presently**	immediately
385	**possessed**	possessed of
386	**son**	son-in-law
389	**I am content**	I accept the terms
395	**ten more**	this would make up the twelve members of a jury – to convict him of murder
402	**gratify**	reward
408	**cope**	give in recompense for
415	**know me**	(pun) recognise me / consider this an introduction / (to Bassanio) treat me as a wife
443	**hold out enemy**	remain an enemy

CHECK THE FILM

Justice is often represented as a woman blindfolded and holding scales and a sword. In this scene, most stage and film versions give the knife and the balance visual prominence.

SCENE 2

- Venice: The wives regain their rings.

Gratiano gives Bassanio's ring to Portia. Nerissa resolves to get back the ring she had given to Gratiano.

COMMENTARY

In this brief scene a good deal of plotting and action is simply conveyed to the audience. The skilful management of Portia and Nerissa is also demonstrated with deft economy. In keeping with the comedy genre conventions of the time, any wrongs that have been committed will be forgiven by the end of the play. When, at the end of Act IV, Scene 2, Portia tells Nerissa that 'we shall have old swearing. That they did give the rings away to men. But we'll outface them, and outswear them too,' (IV.2.15–17) we anticipate a light hearted display of Portia's wit, not a costly battle of wills.

GLOSSARY

5	**you are well o'ertane**	I'm glad to have overtaken you
6	**more advice**	thinking further
11	**my youth**	i.e., Nerissa
15	**old**	plenty of
18	**where I will tarry**	the place where I'll await you

CONTEXT

'The moon shines bright' (V.1.1) is the keynote of an extraordinary exchange between Lorenzo and Jessica which adds nothing to plot but transforms the mood redirecting the play from contest in Venice to Belmont and romance. See **Extended commentaries, text 3**.

ACT V

SCENE 1

- Belmont: All is put right.

After Jessica and Lorenzo's duet, the arrival of Portia and Nerissa is announced; music greets them. When they return, the husbands are upbraided for giving the rings away. All are reconciled after Antonio swears upon his soul that Bassanio will never again break faith, and the ladies restore the rings. A letter tells that three of Antonio's ships are come to harbour. Lorenzo and Jessica learn of Shylock's will. The three couples go off.

COMMENTARY

Formally the lovers' exchange is in marked contrast with everything in the play so far, except the song before Bassanio chooses the leaden casket. It is like an operatic duet about the beauty of the moonlit night as a setting for love. The lovers almost sing the names of the most famous lovers in literature.

High artifice is interrupted by an announcement, and Lancelot brings them down to earth, but Lorenzo returns us to moonlight, the heavens, and the music of the spheres. Music plays. The heroine enters and adds a final poetic aria.

This dose of romantic magic allows the mock-crisis of the broken promises and the revelation of identity to lead to the proper conclusion to both the romance and the comedy. This night is their wedding night.

Antonio, the Merchant, is (magically) restored to fortune, and his pledge of his soul for Bassanio's future fidelity plays a part in the final reconciliation.

GLOSSARY

4	**Troilus** Trojan prince parted from his love Cressida: a scene from Book 5 of Chaucer's poem *Troilus and Criseyde*

GLOSSARY

7	**Thisbe** lover of Pyramus in Chaucer's *Legend of Good Women*; frightened by a **lion**, she failed to make her rendezvous with Pyramus (a scene played in *A Midsummer Night's Dream*)
10	**Dido** lover of Aeneas, who left her at Carthage to found Rome; the **willow** is symbolic of deserted love; also from Chaucer's *Legend*
11	**waft** waved, beckoned
13	**Medea** witch who helped Jason to win the Golden Fleece (Act I.1.169 and III.2.240), also in the *Legend*; but her rejuvenation of Jason's father **Aeson** is from Ovid's *Metamorphoses*
15	**steal** creep away
16	**unthrift** thriftless, prodigal
17	**Stealing** (pun) enticing / saving
21	**shrew** sharp-tongued woman
23	**outnight** outdo in nocturnal comparisons
31	**holy crosses** wayside crosses
33	**hermit** (this is a fictional cover story)
39	**Sola** hunting cry
	Wo ha, ho a falconer's call
46	**post** courier
	horn carried by couriers, but here a horn of plenty also
49	**expect** await
50	**no matter** not so (emphatic)
53	**your music** your musicians
57	**Become** befit
	touches strains
59	**patens** small golden dishes, used for the host at Holy Communion
60	**orb** star
61	**his motion** its orbit
62	**Still choiring** always singing together
	young-eyed cherubins junior angels with piercing sight
63	**immortal souls** (human as well as angelic)
64	**this muddy ... decay** this earthly body
65	**Doth grossly close it** the soul.
66	**Diana** the moon (who 'sleeps with Endymion', line 108)

CONTEXT

In the geocentric cosmos inherited from the Greeks, each planet is set in a crystal sphere guided by an order of angels, each sphere giving a musical note as it revolves. The cosmos makes a harmony which our immortal souls cannot normally hear on earth. The stars have a fixed sphere which forms the floor of heaven.

CONTEXT

In the comedy of *The Merchant of Venice* the noncomic material is pathetic rather than tragic. The happy ending is muted by sympathy for Shylock, and perhaps Antonio, but tragedy requires us to admire, not pity, the protagonist.

GLOSSARY

72	**race** herd
	unhandled unbroken
77	**mutual** common
79	**the poet** Ovid in *Metamorphoses*
80	**Orpheus** the first poet
81	**stockish** blockish (the trees)
	full of rage enraged (the floods)
82	**his** its
85	**spoils** plunder. The line applies to Shylock, who at II.5.29 dislikes the 'vile squealing' of the fife
87	**Erebus** in classical legend, the dark region between earth and the underworld
91	**naughty** wicked
98	**music** musicians
99	**without respect** without context and relationship
103	**attended** expected
109	**Peace, ho!** cease your music
115	**speed** prosper
119–20	**take No note** make no remark
	tucket flourish on a trumpet
122	**his trumpet** only noblemen had tuckets, and each was unique; Bassanio is Lord of Belmont
127–8	**We should hold … sun** your presence turns our night into day, so that we have our day when they do on the other side of the globe
129	**be light** behave wantonly
132	**But God sort all!** let all be as God shall dispose
136	**in all sense** in reason
138	**acquitted of** requited for
141	**breathing courtesy** courteous language
142	**By yonder moon** an inconstant thing to swear by
144	**gelt** gelded
148	**poesy** motto inscribed on the inside of the ring
149	**cutler's poetry** a knife-maker's motto
156	**respective** regardful
159	**and if** if
162	**scrubbèd** shrub-like (in height)

GLOSSARY

176	And 'twere to me if it were to me
199	virtue special quality
206	ceremony sacred symbol
214	held up preserved
220	candles of the night stars
226	liberal free
230	Lie not … home sleep not one night away from home
	Argus the hundred-eyed watchman of classical legend
234	be well advised beware
237	pen (pun) pen / penis
246	of credit worthy of belief (a sarcasm)
252	upon the forfeit be the penalty
253	advisedly knowingly
263–4	the mending … In summer i.e., remedying something which has not gone wrong
266	amazed bewildered
275	Unseal this letter (a theatrical miracle; and Portia miraculously knows its contents)
286	life and living cf. Shylock at IV.1.371–2
288	road anchorage
294	manna food miraculously provided in the desert (Exodus 16:15)
296–7	not satisfied Of not yet heard all about
298	charge us … inter'gatories require us to answer specific questions (Portia reverts to legal jargon)
301	Nerissa's ring a final bawdy joke from Gratiano, since 'ring' could mean 'vulva'

CONTEXT

The last word, given to the ribald Gratiano, has a rude or 'bawdy' second sense. Shakespeare can lower the tone with bawdy at points that can seem inappropriate. He wrote for a popular audience, and the Globe stood next to brothels or 'bawdy houses.'

EXTENDED COMMENTARIES

The analysis of Text 1 concentrates chiefly on character, of Text 2 on theme, and of Text 3 on poetic language.

TEXT 1 – I.3.1–45

Enter BASSANIO *with* SHYLOCK *the Jew*

SHYLOCK: Three thousand ducats, well.

BASSANIO: Ay, sir, for three months.

SHYLOCK: For three months, well.

BASSANIO: For the which, as I told you, Antonio shall be bound.

SHYLOCK: Antonio shall become bound, well.   5

BASSANIO: May you stead me? Will you pleasure me? Shall I know your answer?

SHYLOCK: Three thousand ducats for three months, and Antonio bound.

BASSANIO: Your answer to that?   10

SHYLOCK: Antonio is a good man –

BASSANIO: Have you heard any imputation to the contrary?

SHYLOCK: Ho no, no, no, no: my meaning in saying he is a good man is to have you understand me that he is sufficient. Yet his means are in supposition: he hath an argosy bound to Tripolis, 15 another to the Indies; I understand moreover upon the Rialto he hath a third at Mexico, a fourth for England, and other ventures he hath squandered abroad. But ships are but boards, sailors but men; there be land rats, and water rats, water thieves and land thieves – I mean pirates – and then there is the peril of waters, 20 winds and rocks. The man is notwithstanding sufficient. Three thousand ducats; I thinkI may take his bond.

BASSANIO: Be assured you may.

SHYLOCK: I will be assured I may; and that I may be assured, I will bethink me – may I speak with Antonio?   25

BASSANIO: If it please you to dine with us –

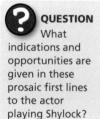

QUESTION
What indications and opportunities are given in these prosaic first lines to the actor playing Shylock?

SHYLOCK: Yes, to smell pork, to eat of the habitation which your
prophet the Nazarite conjured the devil into. I will buy with
you, sell with you, talk with you, walk with you, and so
following; but I will not eat with you, drink with you, nor pray
with you. What news on the Rialto? Who is he comes here?   30

Enter ANTONIO

BASSANIO: This is Signor Antonio.

SHYLOCK: [*Aside*] How like a fawning publican he looks!
I hate him for he is a Christian; But more, for that in low
simplicity   35
He lends out money gratis, and brings down
The rate of usance here with us in Venice.
If I can catch him once upon the hip,
I will feed fat the ancient grudge I bear him.
He hates our sacred nation, and he rails   40
Even there where merchants most do congregate
On me, my bargains, and my well-won thrift
Which he calls interest. Cursèd be my tribe
If I forgive him!

BASSANIO: Shylock, do you hear?

SHYLOCK: I am debating of my present store …   45

The function of the scene is, first, **exposition** of the terms of the
bond, and then of the antipathy between Jew and Christian.
Language and dialogue establish Shylock's character, and the theme of
forgiveness. Stage by stage, Shylock's nature is dramatically revealed.

In the opening exchange as Shylock and Bassanio walk on (lines
1–30), terms are repeated, and characters contrasted: old
businessman and noble young client. Repetition gets the terms into
our heads. Shylock is wary, Bassanio wordy (as with Antonio in Act
I Scene 1). The repetition of 'three' is echoed in Bassanio's triple
question (lines 5–6). Shylock repeats the terms in a formula rather
than answering yes or no. He plays cat and mouse: when Bassanio
presses his question, Shylock turns to discussing Antonio. He seems
unwilling; only later do we learn that he is excited at this chance to
catch Antonio. Although quiet and simple, the opening creates
curiosity and suspense.

CONTEXT

In the Old Testament, pigs are prohibited to Jews as 'unclean' animals: not only inedible, but also unfit for ritual sacrifice because they divide the hoof, admitting excrement into contact with their flesh; they are unfit for God or man.

In a longer speech at line 12 he considers Antonio as a business proposition: he is 'good' (= 'sufficient'), even if his money is all at sea: 'I *may* take his bond'. Bassanio presses; Shylock asks to see Antonio, Bassanio asks him to dinner, Shylock refuses. Caution gives way to passion with: 'Yes, to smell pork.' This sardonic outburst associates Jesus with pork, the smell of which is offensive to Orthodox Jews. Jesus of Nazareth is 'your prophet' not, as Christians believe, the Son of God. Thus Shylock refuses the invitation with an insult. He lists with mounting anger what Jewish Law says he may and may not do: trade or talk with Gentiles, but not eat or pray with them. He gives physical expression to the revulsion he feels for Christians: smell and food express religion and race. He is revealed as a smouldering, passionate man. The different ways in which the moneylender and the gentleman look at things is also a theme: the glamorous 'argosies' of Act I Scene 1 are reduced to physical and financial risks: 'Ships are but boards.' (Ironically, he agrees in Act II to eat with Christians, and he finally prays to their Duke [IV.1.391].)

Shylock's aside (a remark unheard by others onstage) makes plain what before was implied (unless dress and manner have told us already that he is the villain). The aside is a convention by which the dramatist tells the audience of motives hidden from other characters. Shylock's revulsion at the sight of Antonio is expressed in the word 'publican', a tax-collector who took money from fellow Jews. 'I hate him for he is a Christian' makes clear, before Shylock meets Antonio, that he hates him on religious grounds, but *more* as a business enemy. As Shylock goes on, it is hard to tell whether he is more a usurer than a Jew. He wants to 'catch [Antonio] once *upon the hip*' (a biblical phrase, used against him later by Gratiano).

The 'ancient grudge' felt by 'our sacred nation' is identified with financial rivalry: Antonio's widely advertised contempt for 'our thrift / Which he calls interest' is matched by Shylock's commercial contempt for lending money 'gratis' (see Historical Background, on Usury). How would the audience react to the argument that Antonio's practice brings down the rate of usury that Jews can charge in Venice? The connection between religious/ethnic identity and the play's moral theme is summed up in 'Cursèd be my tribe / If I forgive him!'

At this point we know that Shylock hates Christians and has formed a malicious plan to 'catch' Antonio, before he meets him; he will not forgive. His more personal motive for hating Antonio appears later in this scene. He first appears as different, cautious; then as one who takes and gives offence; and finally as consumed with revenge.

His ill-feeling comes out in a prose tirade to Bassanio; the sight of Antonio brings a passionate verse declaration. Antonio does not acknowledge the Jew, who speaks openly to the audience, but not to his enemy.

TEXT 2 – IV.1.359–96

PORTIA: ... Down, therefore, and beg mercy of the Duke.

GRATIANO: Beg that thou mayst have leave to hang thyself –   360
And yet, thy wealth being forfeit to the state,
Thou hast not left the value of a cord;
Therefore thou must be hanged at the state's charge.

DUKE: That thou shalt see the difference of our spirit,
I pardon thee thy life before thou ask it.   365
For half thy wealth, it is Antonio's;
The other half comes to the general state,
Which humbleness may drive unto a fine.

PORTIA: Ay, for the state, not for Antonio.

> **QUESTION**
> The trial scene brings suspense, not justice.' Discuss.

SHYLOCK: Nay, take my life and all, pardon not that: 370
You take my house when you do take the prop
That doth sustain my house; you take my life
When you do take the means whereby I live.

PORTIA: What mercy can you render him, Antonio?

GRATIANO: A halter gratis – nothing else, for God's sake.   375

ANTONIO: So please my lord the Duke and all the court
To quit the fine for one half of his goods,
I am content, so he will let me have
The other half in use, to render it
Upon his death unto the gentleman   380
That lately stole his daughter.

Two things provided more: that for this favour
He presently become a Christian;
The other, that he do record a gift,
Here in the court, of all he dies possessed   385
Unto his son Lorenzo and his daughter.

DUKE: He shall do this, or else I do recant
The pardon that I late pronouncèd here.

PORTIA: Art thou contented, Jew? What dost thou say?

SHYLOCK: I am content.

PORTIA: Clerk, draw a deed of gift.   390

SHYLOCK: I pray you give me leave to go from hence;
I am not well. Send the deed after me
And I will sign it.

DUKE: Get thee gone, but do it.

GRATIANO: In christening shalt thou have two godfathers:
Had I been judge, thou shouldst have had ten more,   395
To bring thee to the gallows, not to the font.

Exit [Shylock]

CONTEXT

Much depends on how director and actor play this scene of Shylock's defeat, and how his 'I am not well' is interpreted.

This is the grand climax of the trial and of the play, focusing on the central conflict of justice and mercy. The pound of flesh has escaped Shylock, and he has just heard that the penalty for attempted murder is death and forfeit of goods. Portia ends with a command to beg for mercy. Does Shylock kneel?

Gratiano jokes that Shylock will have to beg for a rope to hang himself since he will have no money to buy one. A jester and cheerful loud-mouth before the trial, Gratiano is now a scoffer. His voice is that of a wise-cracking spectator at a mass sport (bear-baiting was popular at the time). What would its effect be on the original spectators in The Theatre? Would all react alike? Famous theatrical scoffers were the Jews and to a lesser extent the Romans who in medieval Passion Plays taunted Jesus at his trial and crucifixion. The trial here may be a reversal or **parody** of that trial. ('Parody': an imitation of the style of a well-known work, exaggerating its features for comic purposes.) It is essential to understand the exact terms of what follows.

Ignoring Gratiano, the Duke pardons Shylock's life 'before thou ask it'. He points out that Christians forgive without being asked. This is an illustration not of the Duke's character, but of the play's theme: 'the quality of mercy' is that it is not 'strained' (= constrained, bound) but free, gratis. He repeats the financial penalties: half to the state, half to the intended victim. If Shylock is humble (and asks forgiveness like a Christian), the state's share will be reduced. Portia now puts the ball in Antonio's court.

Shylock's reaction to Christian mercy is indignant: he would rather not be pardoned; he would prefer death to losing his money, for his money is his living, his life. 'House' can mean family, tribe; also private or business house. There is spirit in his reaction, but what else does it reveal?

Ignoring Shylock's defiance, Portia asks Antonio if he can match the Duke's forgiveness. Gratiano repeats his hanging joke, bringing farce into the serious proceedings. (The *Merchant* is a comedy, but Shakespeare puts jokes even into tragedies; the addition of 'for God's sake' is blatantly inappropriate, since Jesus forgave those who put him to death. The joke may also recall that, after betraying Jesus in return for money, Judas 'went and hanged himself' (Luke 27:5).) Ignoring Gratiano's foolery, Antonio speaks to the Duke with a composed courtesy remarkable in one who has just escaped the knife.

Antonio respects court procedure, asking the Duke to let Shylock off the state's half of Shylock's goods on condition that the other half, due to him, is accepted by him only as a non-profit-making trustee for Lorenzo and Jessica. He makes two further immediate conditions: that Shylock become a Christian; and that he make a will leaving everything to his daughter and her husband. The Duke imposes these conditions on penalty of life, and Shylock (after a silence?) accepts them.

Antonio's complex offer shows clemency. He refuses to make money out of Shylock's crime, and insists that the father's money goes to the daughter of his house. However, she has joyfully escaped from the house of bondage and is said to have prodigally wasted Shylock's 'Christian ducats' and family jewels. Her Christian husband will after Shylock's death be legal owner of the

 CHECK THE NET
Look for 'Shakespeare' at the Public Record Office (http://www.pro.gov.uk/virtualmuseum) shows his will, in his own writing, with modern transcription.

CHECK THE FILM

How should Shylock leave? Content to have got off lightly? A broken man? Or a humbled and wiser man? Will he live long? The pathos of Shylock's forced conversion is the climax of Jonathan Miller's BBC TV production of 1980, and of the 2004 film with Al Pacino as Shylock.

wealth that remains. The conditions are generous; but they very sharply fit the crime.

Portia says little but skilfully directs all the proceedings. She asks for Shylock's reply. It is brief: 'I am content.' Even more surprising, he follows with: 'I pray you give me leave …' – a change of tone. He is quiet and monosyllabic as he begs to leave. The Duke allows it, and Gratiano has a final jest.

What are we to make of Shylock's surrender and change of tone? The Christian terms are merciful – if you are a Christian, as Shakespeare and his audience were. A Jew would notice that Shylock is unwilling to die for his religion. Has all his talk been tribal rather than religious? Is the 'prop' of his house his livelihood, his daughter or his religion? On the other side, Shakespeare complicates the issue by having Antonio call Lorenzo 'the gentleman / That lately *stole* his daughter'; we remember Jessica throwing down the casket. Antonio thinks of her future, and the Duke is dignified and unvindictive. The language and the verse of the Christians (apart from the yelps of Gratiano) are measured, courteous and civil. But they get back (eventually) all the money Shylock has made out of them. The financial aspect may also be hinted at in the word 'use' (= trust, in contrast to Shylock's 'usury'). The sentence has two sides, like much in Shakespeare.

Forced conversion offends against modern liberal – and religious – principle. But conversion was, according to Christian belief of the day, a prerequisite of salvation: it is therefore (paradoxically) charity. Antonio, who spat at Shylock, has been humbled, and he now returns good for Shylock's evil.

TEXT 3 – V.1.1-65

Enter LORENZO *and* JESSICA

LORENZO: The moon shines bright. In such a night as this,
When the sweet wind did gently kiss the trees,
And they did make no noise, in such a night
Troilus methinks mounted the Troyan walls
And sighed his soul toward the Grecian tents,   5
Where Cressid lay that night.

JESSICA: In such a night
Did Thisbe fearfully o'ertrip the dew,
And saw the lion's shadow ere himself,
And ran dismayed away.

    LORENZO: In such a night
Stood Dido with a willow in her hand   10
Upon the wild sea banks, and waft her love
To come again to Carthage.

    JESSICA: In such a night
Medea gathered the enchanted herbs
That did renew old Aeson.

    LORENZO: In such a night
Did Jessica steal from the wealthy Jew   15
And with an unthrift love did run from Venice
As far as Belmont.

    JESSICA: In such a night
Did young Lorenzo swear he loved her well,
Stealing her soul with many vows of faith,
And ne'er a true one.

    LORENZO: In such a night   20
Did pretty Jessica (like a little shrew)
Slander her love, and he forgave it her.

JESSICA: I would outnight you, did nobody come:
But hark, I hear the footing of a man.

Enter [STEPHANO,] *a messenger*

LORENZO: Who comes so fast in silence of the night?   25

STEPHANO: A friend.

LORENZO: A friend? What friend? Your name, I pray you, friend?

STEPHANO: Stephano is my name, and I bring word
My mistress will before the break of day
Be here at Belmont. She doth stray about   30
By holy crosses where she kneels and prays
For happy wedlock hours.

LORENZO: Who comes with her?

> **CONTEXT**
>
> Drama had a low reputation. In 1612 Sir Thomas Bodley instructed librarians at his Library in Oxford not to collect it: 'some plays may be worth the keeping, but hardly one in forty'.

Text 3 – V.1.1-63 continued

STEPHANO: None but a holy hermit and her maid.
I pray you, is my master yet returned?

LORENZO: He is not, nor we have not heard from him.   35
But go we in, I pray thee, Jessica,
And ceremoniously let us prepare
Some welcome for the mistress of the house.

Enter [LANCELOT,] *the Clown*

LANCELOT: Sola, sola! Wo ha, ho! Sola, sola!

LORENZO: Who calls?   40

LANCELOT: Sola! Did you see Master Lorenzo? Master Lorenzo,
sola, sola!

LORENZO: Leave holloaing, man! Here!

LANCELOT: Sola! Where, where?

LORENZO: Here!   45

LANCELOT: Tell him there's a post come from my master, with his
horn full of good news: my master will be here ere morning,
sweet soul.

LORENZO: Let's in and there expect their coming.
And yet no matter: why should we go in?   50
My friend Stephano, signify I pray you,
Within the house, your mistress is at hand,
And bring your music forth into the air.

[Exit Stephano]

How sweet the moonlight sleeps upon this bank!
Here will we sit, and let the sounds of music   55
Creep in our ears; soft stillness and the night
Become the touches of sweet harmony.
Sit, Jessica. Look how the floor of heaven
Is thick inlaid with patens of bright gold.
There's not the smallest orb which thou behold'st   60
But in his motion like an angel sings,
Still choiring to the young-eyed cherubins.
Such harmony is in immortal souls,
But whilst this muddy vesture of decay
Doth grossly close it in, we cannot hear it.   65

CHECK THE BOOK

Shylock on the Stage, by Toby Lelyveld, 1960, is scholarly theatre history.

The lovers' conversation is in the musical form of a variation on a theme. The theme is 'The moon shines bright. In such a night as this…' (a line which itself has internal rhyme). Line 3 ends, 'in such a night' and the newly weds speak alternate speeches beginning 'In such a night' in lines 6, 9, 12, 14 and 16. They echo one another like cooing pigeons, or lovers in an opera. Each gives an instance of a silent night-scene from a famous classical love story. Moonlit nights and famous love stories create a romantic atmosphere, and the function of the scene is to change the key and the mood away from the drama of the trial towards the light-hearted 'trial' of Bassanio by Portia and Gratiano by Nerissa, ending in loving reconciliation.

CHECK THE BOOK
Geoffrey Chaucer's *Troilus and Criseyde* tells of Troilus, and his *Legend of Good Women* of Thisbe, Dido and Medea. See Ann Thompson, *Shakespeare's Chaucer: A Study in Literary Origins*, 1978.

The verse is blank (i.e., unrhymed), yet has 'in such a night' seven times, and rhymes 'dew' unromantically with 'Jew' and 'shrew'. The lines move smoothly and regularly, and employ patterns usually found only in nondramatic verse. A string of paired sounds repeats the pattern of the duet: 'no noise', 'Troilus … Troyan', 'sighed his soul', 'Dido … willow', 'wild … waft', 'come … Carthage', 'Jessica … Jew', 'Lorenzo … loved'. Each speech contains a lover's name or two, all taken from Ovid. The first three, also found in Chaucer, are unhappy stories of parted lovers: Cressid had to leave Troilus; Pyramus killed himself after mistakenly thinking Thisbe dead; Dido was deserted by Aeneas. Medea, an enchantress whose magic helped Jason to regain the Golden Fleece from her own father (see III.2.239), here renews her lover's aged father with a very powerful magic brew. This does not seem to go with the first three pairs, except that Medea robbed her father, like Jessica; she later deserted Jason. Aeson was old, and so is Shylock in the next instance, where a young witch 'gathers' something. She 'steals' (creeps away), but also steals gold which makes their 'unthrift' love a more thriving business. Jessica's response to her husband's teasing is that if she stole from her father, Lorenzo stole her soul from her with vows which were all untrue. Lorenzo forgives her; she says she could 'outnight' him but that someone is coming.

The names are famous, melodious and decorative, and that is probably their main function. They change the mood and prepare us for the introduction of music. An educated hearer or reader might, however, have reflected that, as well as love and silence, each instance has an element of unhappiness or infidelity. After Medea,

CHECK THE BOOK

Deborah Cartmell, *Interpreting Shakespeare on Screen*, 2000, is a good introduction.

Lorenzo switches teasingly to Jessica, and Jessica teases him back. With 'little shrew', romance gives way to good humour. There are serious touches: Medea helped Jason win the Golden Fleece, and Portia too is a kind of enchantress who helps her Jason strike gold, though with white rather than black magic. The financial theme is recalled again with 'wealthy' and 'unthrift'. Finally, Lorenzo steals Jessica's soul, with lovers' vows (proverbially false) but also persuades her Jewish soul to become a Christian soul; marital vows must be true. These themes give way to the main business of the scene: wives showing their husbands Christian forgiveness for breaking their word.

Stephano's message does not break the mood, maintaining a 'romance' fiction of the holy bride and her pious maid. The shouts and jokes of the clown Lancelot broaden the humour without ruining the atmosphere. The musicians are heralded by a famous set-piece. Like 'The quality of mercy is not strained', 'How sweet the moonlight sleeps on yonder bank' is entirely serious (though it also has the tenderness of the playful and mischievous love duet which precedes it). The Christian Lorenzo instructs his newly Christian bride in the Christian-Platonic doctrine of the music of the spheres. Moonlight, softness and stillness are heralds not to earthly love and kisses but to an immortal celestial harmony beyond the reach of human ears. Eyes, however, can see the stars like 'patens of bright gold'. 'Patens' is a distinctly Christian reference to the small dishes used in the Communion service, which, seen from below, look like the golden bosses in an elaborate Elizabethan ceiling. The marriage of the Jew's daughter to a Christian is a comedic happy ending, pointing heavenwards. Also, in this wealthy play, they are going to inherit Shylock's earthly gold. There is something magical and arbitrary about the way Lorenzo is made such a wise young man in Belmont, but Belmont has had that effect on Bassanio too. At Belmont, the land of metamorphosis, the heartless Gratiano is lucky, and even Antonio has some luck at last.

PART THREE

CRITICAL APPROACHES

COMEDY AND CONVENTION

The Merchant of Venice is one of Shakespeare's sixteen comedies. Comedy is a special kind of play in which the audience would expect to find a certain kind of story, with certain conventions. Drama involves complication and resolution. If tragedy ends in the death of the hero, comedy ends with a restoration of social order, typically in marriage. Although 'comic' means funny, tending to laughter, comedic means obeying the conventions of comedy as a form or genre. The chief of these is a happy resolution, as suggested by the title of *All's Well That Ends Well*, which is, however, not a very funny play. The rule of comedy is that, however serious the confusion, all ends well. The Italian poet Dante (1265–1326) wrote a *Commedia*, a journey through hell to purgatory and up to heaven, which ends well, but does not make its reader laugh.

Although genre (kind, or form) mattered to Shakespeare, he never abided by the classical division of drama into strictly comic and strictly serious. His comedies came increasingly to include problems difficult to resolve, and to take them more seriously; in some 'problem comedies', such as *Measure for Measure*, the final marriages do not resolve the issues of the play. Early in *The Merchant* (I.1.50) mention is made of 'two-headed Janus', both merry and sad, an emblem of the merry and sad masks of comedy and tragedy, and a signal that mixed drama is to come. The play follows many comedic conventions: its setting is urban, its persons mercantile and middle class, it uses prose; there is a clownish comic servant (Gobbo) and a jester (Gratiano); plot confusion arises from disguise and deception, disaster is avoided, complications are resolved, marriages conclude.

The Merchant also follows conventions from **romance**, an ancient form of story full of marvellous adventure, owing much to folk- and fairytale, in which love finds a way: 'Jack shall have Jill, And all shall be well'. In Roman comedy, grasping fathers tried to marry

> **CONTEXT**
>
> 'Tragedies and comedies ... differ thus: in comedies, *turbulenta prima, tranquilla ultima*; in tragedies, *tranquilla prima, turbulenta ultima*: comedies begin in trouble and end in peace; tragedies begin in calms and end in tempest.' (Thomas Heywood, playwright, in 1612)

unwilling daughters to rich old men. Shakespeare's romantic comedy is less harsh and farcical than this, more gentle, make-believe and idealist; it uses verse; sometimes the young lovers – or the audience – learn something along the way. Other comedic conventions are a festive or party atmosphere, with a clown or fool and some use of song. *The Merchant* has all these elements, blended in a complex plot owing much to folktale (the flesh-bond) and fairytale (the princess and the caskets: see Literary Background, on Sources). Shakespeare emphasises comedic patterns by having three marriages, and raising the possibility of a fourth, between Lancelot and a Moorish girl whom he has made pregnant (III.5.30–35). In comedy, situation normally matters more than character, but Shylock's character is developed to such a point that when his wicked plot is foiled we do not laugh at him. Some Elizabethans will have laughed in The Theatre, as the angry Gratiano does. Gratiano would have hanged Shylock; but we are shown the relative clemency of the Duke and Antonio.

THEMES

LOVE, MARRIAGE AND FRIENDSHIP

In romantic comedy, love finds a way round all obstacles. In the literature of the Middle Ages, love gradually became a popular motive for marriage, in addition to the more practical reasons of procreation and keeping property in the family. Shakespeare's romantic comedies lead up to and end with marriages, including one noble marriage. The suitor loves and serves his lady; but after marriage the wife loves and serves the husband. As soon as Bassanio has chosen rightly, Portia calls him Lord: 'her Lord, her governor, her king' (III.2.165), adding 'Myself, and what is mine, to you and yours / Is now converted'. The husband's corresponding obligations are understood rather than expressed here; but the two are 'one flesh'. Portia behaves throughout as an ideal daughter and wife, according to the ideals of the day.

A letter now arrives announcing Antonio's ruin. Bassanio tells Portia, 'I have engaged myself to a dear friend' (II.2.260). Portia offers her fortune: what was hers is his; and what is his is Antonio's. The wedding takes place offstage. The Renaissance ideal of noble

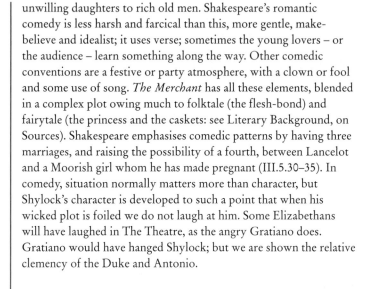

CHECK THE BOOK

The Woman ... shall say 'I (*Name*) take thee (*Name*) to my wedded husband, to have and to hold from this day forward, for better for worse, for richer for poorer, in sickness and in health, to love, cherish, and to obey, till death us do part....'
Then...the Man shall give uno the Woman a Ring and...shall say: 'With this Ring I thee wed, with my body I thee worship, and with all my worldly goods I thee endow.....' (From 'The Solemnization of Matrimony' in *The Book of Common Prayer*, the prayerbook of the Church of England)

friendship between men is less familiar today than the ideal of marriage. Lorenzo praises Portia's 'noble and true conceit / Of god-like amity' (III.4.2–3).

Ideal male friendship is a theme of Renaissance writing; it is called Platonic because first found in the *Phaedrus* of Plato, the Greek philosopher of the fifth century B.C. whose works were revived at the Renaissance. Noble male friendship would be known to the educated from Castiglione's *Book of the Courtier* (1528), translated into English by Sir Thomas Hoby (1561). In the Renaissance idea, this love assumed no active sexual origin or outcome, and was quite compatible with marriage. In Shakespeare's *Sonnets* the older man encourages the younger to marry. Antonio's unconditional love for Bassanio is of this kind, and may owe something to *Il Pecorone*, in which he is the young man's adopted father (see Literary Background, on Sources). Bassanio is introduced to us as Antonio's 'most noble kinsman' (I.1.57), a term which could be used for a godson. In Shakespeare's early play, *Love's Labour's Lost*, he shows how a Platonic Academy based on male friendship breaks down because it underestimates men's need for women; Shakespeare also collaborated in a play with the title *Two Noble Kinsmen*. It is remarkable that neither Portia nor Antonio show any jealousy of the other's love for Bassanio, although Antonio's sadness remains.

MONEY

Money is a theme of the love plot as well as the hate plot of *The Merchant*. Bassanio's need for money to pay court to Portia, 'a lady richly left' (I.1.160), is what puts Antonio in the power of Shylock. Antonio and Shylock are very different merchants, yet all merchants try to make money. And Jessica brings plenty of money with her when she elopes with Lorenzo: she throws down a casket. She then spends extravagantly the money her father had won so carefully. Attitudes to the getting and spending of money are a theme of the play. Wealth does not make Portia happy; she needs to love and be loved. Spending money is more fun than getting it, and generosity is better than meanness. Yet generosity is not the word for a daughter exchanging a turquoise ring for a monkey. Life with Shylock must have been grim, but the ring Jessica steals and then exchanges for a monkey was the ring her mother gave to her father. If Bassanio has been extravagant, Jessica is prodigal; unlike the Prodigal Son, she

> **CONTEXT**
>
> *The Merchant of Venice* is 'citizen comedy', for its characters are middle class. The rank of the Duke, magnificoes, and 'royal merchants' comes from money, not the sword. The 'nobility' of Venice's reputation depended upon its respect for law.

Money continued

does not go back to her father for forgiveness. Is the implication that she has nothing to be ashamed of?

The Elizabethan nobility and gentry needed money to keep up the generosity expected of their rank, but rents from land could not keep up with rampant inflation, still less with the wealth made in the City of London. Gentlemen like Sir Philip Sidney and aristocrats like the Earl of Essex owed huge sums to City merchants – a common topic in Elizabethan writing. The old social hierarchy was under violent strain. Commerce was almost respectable, and moneylending almost acceptable; yet the taking of interest was unpopular and usury, although legal, was still widely regarded as morally wrong (see section on **Usury**). The new merchant venturers, however, who financed international trade as Antonio does, had a certain glamour.

Venice (see **Historical background on Venice**) was a mercantile city, and its luxurious life is based not on land and title but on commerce, law and credit. Although Bassanio has been a prodigal son (or godson), his godfather forgives him and is happy to finance his adventure or 'pilgrimage' to Belmont. Bassanio deserves Portia because he is not taken in by 'outward shows' (III.2.73), the glamour of precious metals; he is granted a moral insight. But Jessica's unfilial theft of her father's gold raises questions. Does her love-scene with Lorenzo in Act V Scene 1 redeem their love? Such a transformation of character could be an allegory of the effect of conversion and of marriage. It is also convenient for dramatic purpose, effacing the trial scene and providing romance for the reunion of Portia and Bassanio.

Portia's wealth is fabulous: she is the Golden Fleece won by Jason, and Belmont is an Eldorado of which Bassanio becomes lord. But Portia's readiness to give her fortune and herself away for love is matched by Antonio's. This loving and giving is in stark contrast to a greed which prefers ducats to a daughter and a hate which prefers a pound of flesh to thousands of ducats. Royal merchants are generous. Yet the association of wealth with glamour and alluring appearance raises questions in the scene of Jessica's elopement. She cheats her father, as Portia does not. Shakespeare parallels these daughters who marry adventurers of various degrees of merit, and

CONTEXT

The Merchant of Venice is full of hierarchy: father/daughter, master/servant, senior/ junior. But the hierarchy of rank is built upon an unstable commerce. The Elizabethan satirist Thomas Nashe wrote that 'The usurer eateth up the gentleman, and the gentleman the yeoman, and all three being devoured one of an-other, do nothing but complain.'

he parallels their engagements. When the joker Gratiano has won Nerissa, he says to Bassanio that 'We are the Jasons' (III.2.240); but he is not Bassanio, and his conduct in the trial scene is neither heroic, gentle nor Christian. Parallelism and silent comparison are favourite techniques of this playwright. Gold rings are tokens of exchange, of wealth, and of engagement; it is worth comparing the fates of the rings belonging to Leah, Nerissa and Portia.

JUSTICE AND MERCY

The keynote of the play is Portia's 'The quality of mercy is not strained' (IV.1.180), in the trial scene. It alerts the audience to what is at issue. Shylock has the right in law to his pound of flesh, and refuses the plea for mercy. He insists on justice, the law, his bond. Portia likewise refuses Bassanio's plea that she should relax the law, knowing that in the exact wording of the bond lies Antonio's salvation. Although every argument and move counts in this trial scene, the trial is dramatic rather than legal. Drama is conflict, and the trial is a contest between two radically opposed attitudes to the human life which is at stake.

Portia's argument for mercy is the Christian one that no-one deserves salvation, for it is only God's mercy that can save a human soul. It does not move Shylock, who demands justice according to the law. Yet Shylock's true motive is not respect for law, but revenge. Jessica says that she has heard him swear to his Jewish friends 'That he would rather have Antonio's flesh / Than twenty times the value of the sum / That he did owe him' (III.2.285–7). On first seeing Antonio, Shylock's first lines are:

> How like a fawning publican he looks.
> I hate him for he is a Christian. (I.3.33–4)

A Christian audience would identify Shylock's attitude here as that of the righteous Pharisee proud of his religious observance who scorns the humble publican who knows he is a sinner (Luke 18: 9–14). Jews were seen by Christians as Pharisees, observers of the old law of Moses, rather than of the new law that Jesus gave, of love for God and of neighbour, and of forgiveness and turning the other cheek. The Gospels often show the Pharisees trying to catch Jesus breaking the letter of the law: as when he declines to condemn the

? QUESTION
Can poetic drama be turned into film, a medium which uses images rather than words, without essential loss?

woman taken in adultery. St Paul also contrasts the Old Law (the Mosaic law) with the New Law of love.

Such a Christian view of Judaism is, however, partial and unfair, for the Jews of the Old Testament relied on the mercy of God, especially in the Psalms, the prayerbook of Jews before it was that of Christians: 'If thou, Lord, shouldest mark us according to our iniquities, O Lord, who shall stand?' (Psalm 130). But Shylock's early speeches are full of the Patriarchs Abraham and Jacob, and of the Law; he speaks of Jews as 'my tribe'. He seems a stiff, tribal and primitive Jew, and does not quote the spiritual wisdom of the Psalms or the Prophets. This would confirm the hostile stereotype, prevalent in Shakespeare's day, of Jews as a separate people, harsh and retaliatory. Shylock's insistence on blood contrasts with Antonio's willingness to lay down his life for his friend, a version of the supreme Christian ideal of love. Antonio forgives Bassanio's prodigality; Shylock cannot forgive Jessica's. The play's fifth act shows women forgiving men for having broken their word and given away their rings, a forgiveness which leads to the reconciliation required by comedy.

Two figures are left out of the reconciliation, Shylock and Antonio. The self-sacrificing Antonio is left alone, with the token consolation of three ships miraculously restored. Shylock's position is discussed in Characterisation below, together with the question of the justice of his punishment.

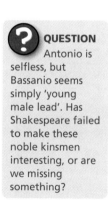

QUESTION
Antonio is selfless, but Bassanio seems simply 'young male lead'. Has Shakespeare failed to make these noble kinsmen interesting, or are we missing something?

CHARACTERISATION

The Merchant of Venice has four leading characters – Antonio, Bassanio, Portia and Shylock – with several minor characters. It should be remembered that although Shakespeare deepens his major characters and gives them a psychology, drama does not allow the fullness of all-round depiction and exploration found in some novels. We learn much of the thoughts of Hamlet and other tragic characters, but less of characters in comedy.

ANTONIO

Antonio is 'sad' (I.1.1 and I.1.94) and unselfish. His noble friendship for his kinsman Bassanio is such that 'He only loves the world for him' (II.8.51). Antonio is a 'royal merchant' (III.2.238) with ships trading to the Levant, England and Mexico: 'argosies with portly sail / Like signors and rich burghers of the flood' (I.1.9–10). The glamour of ships is established by such awestruck comments, but so are the perils of the sea: we hear of spices scattered on the stream and of roaring waters enrobed with silk. Antonio is patient with Bassanio's extravagance and readily agrees to lend him more. His sadness may be a hint of suffering to come.

Shylock declares hatred for Antonio yet addresses him deferentially. Antonio is open about his distaste for Shylock: he breaks a custom in borrowing money at interest; he has rescued those who owed Shylock interest and could not pay. (For the ensuing argument about usury, see section on **Usury**). He admits calling Shylock a misbeliever and a cut-throat dog and spitting on him; he says he would do so again. In his anger, he is surprised by Shylock's offer of friendship, and an interest-free loan; and risks the fantastic penalty of a pound of flesh. Bassanio is suspicious, but Antonio takes the bait, as the plot requires.

In later scenes Antonio is gentle, patient and unselfish. He conceals his sorrow at Bassanio's departure for Belmont, wishing him success. He faces the trial with resignation: 'I am a tainted wether of the flock' (IV.1.114). This may be a cue as to how the audience should see him rather than a revelation of character. He is ready to face death if he can say goodbye to Bassanio. He urges the sending of the ring after Portia. He takes the blame for the quarrel between the lovers in Act V and pledges his soul that Bassanio will be true. He passes the ring to Bassanio; he is left alone at the end.

His treatment of Shylock needs examination: he asks the Duke to let Shylock off the state's share, and declines to takes his half of Shylock's estate except as a trustee for Jessica and Lorenzo. This is consistent with his principle that he does not profit from the misfortunes of others. His conditions are that Shylock leaves his

CHECK THE FILM

In the BBC TV production by Jonathan Miller (1980), the forced conversion of Shylock is brutal: his skull-cap is knocked off and he is forced to kiss a crucifix. Both director and Shylock (Warren Mitchell) are Jewish. There are similar emphases in Al Pacino's Shylock in the 2003 film of the play.

CHECK THE FILM

Shylock's passionate aside (Act I, Scene 3) and his first verse, tells us that he secretly hates Antonio as a Christian and will not forgive him. It was cut in Alan Horrox's production of *The Merchant of Venice*, 1996, directed for Channel 4.

estate to his daughter and becomes a Christian, or his estate is forfeit. Antonio takes nothing.

Difficulties in Antonio's character arise from historical changes in values. In the absence of the Renaissance ideal of noble friendship, Antonio's love for a man might seem homosexual, an opportunity mistakenly taken by some modern directors. The demand that Shylock become a Christian denies liberty of religion. But in 1600 such a liberty was practically unknown, and Christian doctrine was that without conversion Shylock's soul would be damned. In the event, Shylock agrees to give up his religion rather than his living. It is hard to forget Antonio's insults to Shylock, for which he sees no need to apologise. Shylock may be a 'cut-throat' usurer, but he is not a dog and does not deserve to be spat at. We cannot condone Antonio's treatment, for it is a striking exception to his general courtesy and confirms the general rule that Christians in the play taunt Shylock in a way that shows no Christian humility. All this is, however, modified by the mercy shown by Antonio to a man who has tried to kill him.

BASSANIO

Bassanio is a young gentleman, a 'noble kinsman' (I.1.57) of Antonio's, and perhaps (as in the source, *Il Pecorone*) an adopted son, or a godson to the older man. He is embarrassed to ask his old friend Antonio for money, but not ashamed, though he has wasted money that Antonio had already advanced him. Aspiring to marry Portia, he needs money, as young gentlemen often do. The audience might be expected to be almost as indulgent as Antonio.

His theatrical role is that of the young male lead, stylish, enterprising, decent if not heroic. Youth is his leading characteristic: he is impulsive, gallant, generous but slightly immature. He is not a good credit risk: his policy of firing a second arrow to find a first he has lost might not impress a bank manager. But he ventures for Portia, and, at the crucial test, chooses rightly: his instincts are good. He had had the sense to suspect Shylock's 'merry sport' (I.3.172): 'I like not fair terms and a villain's mind' (I.3.138). Compared with the noisy Gratiano, whom he more than generously allows to come with him to Belmont, he is gentle, even noble. His reactions to

Antonio's letter and at the trial are heartfelt; he offers his life (evoking a witty response from Portia), but can do nothing. As Portia's husband, he cannot reciprocate his friend's love, although he defers to Antonio's sense of obligation and gives away Portia's ring. Is he right to do so? He has less presence of mind than his wife. Does that matter? He is the least of the four main players.

PORTIA

Portia's role is that of golden princess, prize and bride in the fairytale casket test; Shakespeare fills Belmont with glamour, wealth, exotic visitors, music and moonlight. He changes the lady of his source from a sexual temptress to a young woman, magical but distinctly human. When she reviews her suitors with Nerissa, she is not just a beautiful and dutiful daughter, but a girl of independent mind, bored, not easily pleased, with a witty tongue, a shrewd judgement and a heart vulnerable to love. She is ceremonious to her grand suitors, yet relieved when they fail. Before Bassanio chooses, she is highly excited and emotional, yet resists the temptation to guide his choice. When his friend's plight is known, she is generous, quick, decisive: he must go to his friend, but marry first. She keeps quiet about her rescue attempt. From passive heroine she becomes active hero. Her performance in the trial (a gift to boy actor and to actress) is masterly, first setting out rights and wrongs ('The quality of mercy is not strained'), then leading Shylock into the written trap into which he had led Antonio. Her skill and touch are no less sure after the trial, as she rapidly manipulates her 'merry sport' in Venice and at Belmont. She has the gifts of an actor-manager, getting the most out of each situation. It seems that Shakespeare has succeeded in the impossible task of making a young, beautiful, clever and rich woman into a virtuous example of selfless love, while persuading us that she is hard-headed, modest, witty and good fun.

QUESTION
'Love is mysterious: the brave and witty Portia obeys as a daughter and a wife, yet has more initiative and brains than her man.' Discuss.

SHYLOCK

Shylock appears in five scenes and speaks less than Bassanio or Portia, yet he dominates, even on the page. The traits of his character are rapidly laid down and repeated: focus on money, hatred of Christians, pride in Jewish identity, caution, calculation, cunning, experience, inflexible will (see **Extended commentaries, text 1**). Our attitude to Shylock varies sharply. We recoil from his

expressed hatred, but when we hear of his treatment by Antonio, we sympathise. He makes Antonio angry, then surprises him with an offer of friendship and an interest-free loan; this has a 'merry' clause, but Antonio takes the bait. We see Shylock's skill as a negotiator; then, his close-fistedness with his servant and possessiveness towards his daughter reveal him as a domestic tyrant. But when Jessica elopes, scattering money and family jewels, we see him taunted by Christians and tortured by Tubal's news. His emotion is intense, and his pain evokes pity, followed by revulsion: for his money-lust is such that he would rather have his daughter lying at his feet, dead, with the money in the coffin and the jewel in her ear: he prefer his ducats to his daughter, as the boys in Venice say. It is a defining moment: disgust kills the sympathy aroused by 'If you prick us, do we not bleed?' (III.1.50–1) and prepares us for its conclusion: 'If you wrong us, shall we not revenge?' (III.1.52). This bloody revenge puts Shylock beyond what Christianity can approve.

His performance at the trial is dominating, unbending, obsessive: he savours the prospect of revenge, exposes the hypocrisy of Christian slave-holding, and dismisses with contempt all pleas for mercy and offers of money. He meets his match in Portia, and when he is surprised, outwitted and prevented from taking his revenge, the audience must have rejoiced. At the climax, with whetted knife raised and the scales waiting, the drama of the moment banishes considerations of character. Our feelings sway as we watch Shylock trying to save 9,000 ducats, then 3,000 ducats, then his dignity. He tries to leave, but must face the penalty for attempting the life of a citizen. He is told to kneel for mercy, and a kind of mercy is extended to him. He says he is 'content' (IV.1.389). The different reactions of Portia, Gratiano, the Duke and Antonio cause us to think about justice rather than character, and we shall not all come to the same conclusions. Shylock leaves quickly, unwell, and we are soon made to think of other things: tricks, disguises, moonlight, music and the renewal of love. But Shylock's fierce emotions trouble the memory as we think over the justice of his fate. Comedies with happy endings can be serious.

Shylock, like Portia, is a character taken from an old story and much changed by Shakespeare. The primitive stage Jew of tradition, a comic villain, is given human feelings and pride of family, unlike Marlowe's Jew of Malta. This Jew is no longer a caricature, though he remains the villain of a story where evil is not all on one side. Some of the disagreements over Shylock are due to the **paradox** that he is both the devilish, bloodthirsty wolf that Gratiano thinks him and also the human victim of snubs and vilification which make his revenge understandable: 'The villainy you teach me I will execute' (III.1.56). Most of the disagreements over Shylock come from long-term changes in attitudes since 1600 (see **Critical history**). These changes began at the time of Shakespeare. Jews, Christians, and critics ignorant of religion or indifferent or hostile to it will begin from different viewpoints.

In considering the penalty of the pound of flesh, which may seem incredible today, it is often said that it comes from a primitive or folktale level, implying that this level no longer exists. It should also be remembered that Elizabethan theatre audiences also attended the public executions of enemies of the state, whose offence was sometimes a religious one (Catholic priests, for example, could be executed for saying mass). Execution took the form of hanging, drawing and quartering, in which a skilled executioner, having hanged the man, cut out the heart while the victim was still alive and held it up to the audience. Similarly barbarous forms of judicial killing are still in use in some societies. In her *Out of Africa*, the Danish writer Karen Blixen reports that her African servant, a Somalian Muslim, was outraged by the outcome of Antonio's trial, holding that Shylock had been cheated of his pound of flesh, and that a skilful man could certainly have cut out exactly one pound without shedding blood.

QUESTION
'To understand all is not to pardon all.' Does Shylock's mistreatment by Christians justify his vindictiveness? Discuss.

MINOR CHARACTERS

Characters in plays, and particularly minor characters, sometimes change their roles and their natures to meet the demands of the theatre and of the plot. The most interesting of the many lesser characters in *The Merchant* are Gratiano, Lancelot Gobbo, Lorenzo and Jessica. Gratiano 'plays the Fool' (I.1.79) to Antonio's young friends: he is a mocker, a noisy talker, a gentleman-clown. His role is partly derived from the comic Vice of the Morality Plays, the tempter-entertainer. As Bassanio's second, he wins Portia's lady-in-waiting Nerissa (boasting 'We are the Jasons' (III.2.240)) and loses the ring she gives him. At the trial, he baits Shylock and demands vengeance. Gratiano is often a foil to deeper characters, bringing out by contrast Antonio's sadness, Bassanio's discretion, and the mercy of the nobler Venetians. He has the last word, a bawdy joke. On the other hand, his moral critique of affected gravity is reasonable (though Antonio's sadness is real, not affected), and his 'How like a younger or a prodigal' (II.6.15) is a key speech of the play.

The stage-direction for Lancelot Gobbo on his first appearance reads 'Enter Clown'. With his comic Anglo-Italian name, his role is a traditional one, written for the company's professional comedian, Will Kemp. In accordance with comic tradition, he makes cruel fun of his father. Lancelot is an unedifying comic servant whose prose made the audience laugh; a 'wit-snapper' whose comic patter (now rather obscure) includes plays on words, catch-phrases, rude jokes (known as 'bawdy'), **malapropism** and nonsense. He lightens the mood and offsets the tragic potentiality of the plot, although at times he is shrewd. He jokingly admits (in III.5) that he has got a black girl pregnant; but this issue is not followed up in the play.

The lovers Lorenzo and Jessica seem to change their natures after they run away together. At Belmont they are romantic lovers (see **Extended Commentaries, text 3**), but earlier their elopement raises some doubts. When Jessica dares to escape from her father's house of bondage, we sympathise, even when she throws down a 'casket' of his money to Lorenzo, who then praises her as 'wise, fair and true' (II.6.57). Yet on their honeymoon spree, Jessica is rumoured to have given a turquoise in exchange for a monkey. What her father had treasured, she squanders. Lorenzo marries for love *and* money, as does Bassanio; a casket is again involved. Jessica also becomes a Christian, a Gentile, a *gentle* (noble) Venetian. The questions raised by such a conversion are reabsorbed into the comic onrush of the play; but the case of Jessica confirms that the role of minor characters is often to cast light on the themes of the play and the values of others.

STYLE AND LANGUAGE

VERSE DRAMA: PROSE AND POETRY

Like other poetic dramatists of his day, Shakespeare used prose as well as verse. Society was hierarchical, and as the Renaissance theory of decorum or form prescribed, high style dignified kings and tragedy, low style was used for servants and comedy. Shakespeare and his audience shared a sense of linguistic register (high, middle and low areas of the vocabulary). *The Merchant* uses prose for servants, clowns, chat, jokes, realism and comedy; verse for courtiers, ideals and romance. In *The Merchant*, financial terms and quayside gossip are in 'low' prose, whereas the trial is in verse, and courtship in a 'high' formal poetry which is musical.

Verse and music are based on measures of time, unlike prose. Verse is measured prose; song is verse put to music. Modern films, plays and television drama are in prose, and although prose has more than one register, these modern media have other resources. Shakespeare's stage had no scenery or lighting, and he needed the extra resources of verse. Poetic drama is like opera: narrative passages have little or no music; big scenes need more music; the best tunes are reserved for dramatic duets and emotional arias.

Prose and verse intensify contrast when the same thing is shown at different levels. Thus, after Shylock has told in verse how Jacob, helped by his wise mother, fooled his blind father into giving him something which was not his due, we see Lancelot Gobbo getting his blind father to help him get a new position; the comic version is in prose. This parallel might recall a more distant parallel: the prodigal Bassanio getting a loan from a godfather, who is (in worldly terms) blinded by his love for him. Another contrast is that Bassanio asks Antonio for help in verse, while Shylock curses his prodigal daughter in prose. Much of the variety of *The Merchant* comes from the range of stylistic resources at Shakespeare's command. This enables him, after the drama of Shylock's exit, to turn on the maximum poetic power in the loving exchanges between Lorenzo and Jessica in order to recreate the magic of Belmont so that the play can end with the renewal of love.

> **CONTEXT**
>
> Professional funny men are rarely funny out of context. Gobbo is not a Fool, but a clown, whose antics are funnier than his words now seem.

LANGUAGE, IMAGERY AND THEMES

Poetry was once defined by the American poet Ezra Pound as 'bee-yewtiful thoughts in flowery langwidge'. Pound was mocking the monotony of post-Romantic poetry. In this 'bee-yewtiful' sense, Shakespeare was not a poetic dramatist but a language dramatist. He made plays out of all kinds of language. On the stage, romantic poetry is not often called for, even in romantic comedy. The most telling images in *The Merchant* are shocking thoughts in brutal language: Shylock's 'I would my daughter were dead at my foot, and the jewels in her ear,' or his comparison of Antonio to a rat to be poisoned. Some key images of the play are simply phrases which raise questions: 'a royal merchant' (IV.1.29); 'a pound of flesh' (IV.1.322). Thus language is hard to separate from theme. A writer is looking for the right word, not the beautiful word.

LANGUAGE AND CHARACTER-CREATION

Shakespeare opens scenes with words which create character and theme at once. Antonio begins Act I Scene 1: 'In sooth, I know not why I am so sad'. Portia begins Scene 2: 'By my troth, Nerissa, my little body is aweary of this great world'. Shylock opens Scene 3 with 'Three thousand ducats, well', establishing situation as well as character and theme. Lorenzo's first words to Jessica in Act 2 Scene 4 tell us his plan *and* that he is ashamed of it: 'Nay, we will slink away in supper time'. Shylock's calculating repetition of words suggests that to him a word may be a term in a contract (see **Extended commentaries, text 1**). A sense of his different ethnic identity is created early by his speech habits: he speaks of 'my tribe' (I.3.44 and 49) (Jews); he will 'not eat with you' (I.3.30) (Christians). Judaic ritual regulations governing the preparation of food entail separate cooking arrangements, an issue arising in all multi-faith societies. He constantly uses Hebrew names: Jacob, Abraham, Hagar and Leah. His idioms and references are different – either proudly patriarchal, or grossly physical. He speaks of things: jewels, money, sheep, cats, rats, pigs, blood, urine, flesh. The Christians in turn call him a dog, spurn him with their feet, spit on him. To them he is a cur, a wolf, a devil, subhuman. He replies by reminding them of the physical basis of their common humanity: 'If you prick us, do we not bleed?' (III.1.50–1). In return, he wants blood.

CHECK THE BOOK

John Gross's *Shylock: Four Hundred Years in the Life of a Legend*, 1994, is an excellent survey.

SPECIAL LANGUAGE AND ANALOGY

Shylock has his own prose, and uses special Jewish vocabulary which marks him as different. Other special forms of language in the play are Christian and classical. These would not in themselves have seemed special to Shakespeare's audience; educated men read Latin, and everyone went to church on Sunday. It was a Christian society familiar with the Bible from readings at church, and from private reading. The poet whom Shakespeare most often quotes and imitates, however, is the pagan Ovid: his *Metamorphoses*, as a guide to mythology, and his legends of classical lovers. The play is full of analogies or parallels to Christian and classical stories.

CLASSICAL ANALOGIES

These are used for two aspects of the casket plot: Bassanio's adventure to Belmont, and the lavish Ovidian imagery of love scenes, notably the Casket scene and the duet in Act V Scene 1 between Lorenzo and Jessica (discussed in **Extended commentaries, text 3**). Bassanio likens Portia's 'sunny locks' (I.1.68) to the Golden Fleece sought by Jason and his Argonauts, guarded by a dragon. Jason won the Fleece with the help of the magic of Medea, and there is something magic about Belmont and its 'Lady richly left'. She laughingly likens Bassanio to Alcides (in Latin called Hercules), a hero who performed labours such as rescuing a virgin from a sea-monster. Choosing a casket is a test of discrimination rather than of courage, though much depends upon it. When Bassanio has done so, Gratiano claims that 'we are the Jasons, we have won the Fleece' (III.2.240); rather like a Grand Prix winner spraying champagne. But is their adventure heroic, or fortunate (and fortune-bringing)? How does its heroism compare with Portia's rescue of Antonio? Is the true hero of the play Balthazar?

CHECK THE BOOK

Shakespeare took his mythology from Ovid's *Metamorphoses*, which he knew in Latin, also using the 1567 verse translation by Arthur Golding.

CHRISTIAN LANGUAGE

There is more Christian language in *The Merchant* than in any other comedy, partly because of its story of the Jew and the flesh-bond. Shakespeare used the book of Genesis to create an Old Testament religious identity for Shylock; he did not want to leave him as a villain whom we could laugh at when baulked of his prey. He also makes Shylock pointedly anti-Christian: he mocks the New

Testament, with his insulting references to the Nazarite, the Gadarene swine and the publican (see **Extended commentaries, text 1**). He wishes that 'any of the stock of Barabbas' (IV.1.292) had been Jessica's husband rather than a Christian: Barabbas was the thief whom the Jewish mob released, preferring to crucify Jesus. What effect would Shylock's gibes have upon the audience?

Jesus's parable of the Prodigal Son is an evident analogy to the wasteful Bassanio returning to his forgiving (god)father. It is recalled again in the image of the strumpet wind (II.6.15). Forgiveness is a theme of the play (see Justice and Mercy), and so is sacrifice. Some critics see Antonio's willingness to die for Bassanio as a parallel with Christ's willingness to offer himself as the victim at the Paschal feast, taking the sins of mankind upon him, like the scapegoat of the Old Testament. Such parallels between religion and contemporary life were commonplace in drama. But the parallel is partial: Antonio's blood is not spilt, though he offers his soul to reconcile Portia and his beloved Bassanio. A negative parallel is more likely: that we are to see in Shylock's knife and scales reminders both of civil justice and punishment and also of ritual sacrifice, including the threatened sacrifice of Isaac by Abraham in Genesis and the sacrifice of the Paschal Lamb at the Jewish Passover in Exodus. These are to be contrasted with the advice. freely to forgive those who trespass against us, given in Portia's 'The quality of mercy is not strained' (IV.1.180) which alludes to the petition in the Our Father or Lord's Prayer: 'Forgive us our trespasses, as we forgive those who trespass against us.'

CHECK THE BOOK

Frank Kermode, *Shakespeare's Language*, 2000, is attentive to linguistic details such as the relation of 'gentle' to 'gentile' in *The Merchant of Venice*.

WORD PLAY

There are many other kinds of language in *The Merchant*, including Lancelot's nonsense and **malapropism**. But, as often in Shakespeare, there is sense inside some of the nonsense. Shakespeare had a weakness for puns, sometimes known as quibbles. Had Shakespeare wished to avoid them, puns were harder to avoid in writing Elizabethan English than they are in modern English, since spelling was not yet standardised. Shakespeare spelled his own name in different ways. Modern editions of Shakespeare modernise spelling and punctuation. Dr Johnson said that 'A quibble was to Shakespeare the fatal Cleopatra for which he lost the world and was content to lose it.' Johnson thought a pun a low form of humour, and that a cheap pun sacrificed all seriousness. But Shakespeare's idea of **decorum** was much less rigid; he often makes a serious point with a weak play on words. Indeed he plays on the last word in the play.

PART FOUR

CRITICAL HISTORY

Apart from theoretical and political approaches, three scholarly approaches have altered our understanding of Shakespeare recently: bibliography; stage history; and the history of critical reception.

BIBLIOGRAPHY

QUESTION
'He was not of an age, but for all time,' Ben Jonson wrote of Shakespeare. How far is a director justified in adapting a Shakespeare play to the concerns of the present day?

Bibliography, the physical study of the printing of the texts in order to get closer to what Shakespeare wrote, does not much affect *The Merchant*, for its existing texts hardly differ: Shylock is sometimes 'Jew' in speech-prefixes, and sometimes 'Shylock'. And if the quarto edition's title page advertises 'the extreme crueltie of *Shylocke* the Iewe', these are the words of a bookseller, not of the author. Guesses at Shakespeare's attitudes have to be based on his writings. All we have is a play-text, close to that of early performances.

STAGE HISTORY

If we turn to stage history, the early record is scanty. It was performed 'divers times' before 1600, probably in 1596–7; and then at court before James I in 1605. The king asked for it again two days later, on Shrove Tuesday, the festive day before Lent. We hear of no further performance until 1741, although in 1701 it was used as the basis of *The Jew of Venice* by Granville, much cut and rewritten, with Shylock as comic villain, but as the focal figure. In 1741 a more restored version, with Shylock as a fierce villain, began the play's popularity. In 1814 Kean made Shylock more humane. Various versions then held the stage, cut and adapted to suit the needs of a changing theatre, including the unchanging need for money. The actor Henry Irving privately described Shylock as 'a bloody-minded monster'. But that is not how he chose to play Shylock in his lavish revival of the play with Ellen Terry as Portia in 1879. His own Shylock returned home in Act II to knock on the door of an empty house; and Act V was dropped. Shylock was the 'type of a persecuted race; almost the only gentleman in the play, and most ill-used.' Portia was womanly — not an option in 1597 — and full of warmth. Irving's version ran for 250 nights.

Theatre people have not usually felt obliged to respect Shakespeare's words, though his works have been a source of box-office income for nearly four centuries. His play-texts were freely rewritten and adapted until about the 1760s, when there arose a cult of 'the Bard', as he came to be known (not a title to be used seriously today). This 'Bardolatry' led to a veneration of Shakespeare among the Romantics, a cult which continues, and can go stale. Yet it was not until the twentieth century that fidelity to the language of the text, and respect for the author's presumed intentions, became priorities, as they had always been for scholars and schoolteachers. Shakespeare has for centuries furnished raw material to the businesses connected to the theatre, historical scholarship, educational publishing, and global tourism: thousands of people have made their living out of Shakespeare. Yet the scholarly pursuit of accurate texts and historically authentic staging has always had to compete with cultural and political fashion, and with the vanity and egotism of those actors and directors who wish to turn a classic into an image of themselves. Since the 1970s the fashion in British theatre has been anti-establishment. Egotism is not unknown in academic criticism: a tendentious reading can be fastened upon a play in order to recommend a political, social or sexual agenda. A different theatrical tendency, thanks to the place of Shakespeare in the school curriculum and also to his popularity with foreign tourist groups who cannot understand his English, has been to try to simplify the language, the characters and the ideas of a play while enlivening its action, a tendency noticeable in productions at the reconstructed Globe.

The Victorian production had Shylock as a comic villain in a red wig, a usurer whose Jewishness is incidental. An Antonio of 1932 was a decadent and his friends bourgeois idlers. In 1933 Hitler came to power, since when Shylock has not often been the villain of the piece. In 1970 Jonathan Miller produced a gentlemanly assimilated Jew (Laurence Olivier), cutting 'I hate him for he is a Christian'. Jewish directors and actors usually make his Jewishness central; yet he can be a Jew of different kinds, dignified or undignified: an unassimilated oriental Jew; a central European Jew with a Yiddish accent; or a Jew who is content to change his religion if he can keep some money. The first of these can be found in the text. But the text has nothing to say about some things. Settings can be Elizabethan,

? QUESTION
Does it make much difference to our idea of *The Merchant* that all the original actors were male?

Victorian, or modern Italian; Antonio can be made openly homosexual; swastikas can be painted on the walls. What works in the theatre depends on time, place and fashion. In Nazi Germany the play was used as anti-Jewish propaganda. That is not the way it is done in modern Germany or New York or Israel, or in Australia or Japan, or modern England.

Stage history suggests that the millions of people who have seen the play since James I have rarely heard all the words in the texts we read. The stage does not have a literary critic's respect for the text. It is only a script for acting; if the text presents a problem, it can be changed or cut. Stage history shows that over four centuries any cultural phenomenon will change a good deal. If by some miracle the performance James I saw were put on at the 'authentic' 1996 Globe, or at a reconstruction of The Theatre, the audience would not be authentic Jacobeans. The play James I saw would seem different to them, and it would thereby become a rather different play.

QUESTION
If you were directing the play and had to cut it to a performance of two hours, what would you cut, and why?

It is not only theatre-goers who have changed. Those who read the play without seeing it have also changed. But they read the text rather than have the theatre interpret it for them. A careful reading of the text can prevent the more perverse kinds of misinterpretation. Yet there is no single right reading of a play, for it dramatises several voices, none of them the author's. A play is like a tennis match without an umpire; there is no superior fixed viewpoint.

Today, many people, not only students, may be more likely to see a film, video or TV version of *The Merchant of Venice* than a stage version. The consequences need to be thought about.

Schools use videos and DVDs, and the recorded visual version may come to rival the text tudied in class. Video and DVD have the benefit that a scene or a dramatic moment can be slowed down and re-run and studied. But the plays were written for the theatre, not for the large or the small screen, and should be seen on stage if at all possible. Filmed versions have a finished fixity which is quite different to the unpredictable life of a text in stage performance, where the communal imaginative experience has a shared impact for the audience quite unlike the private viewing of a video. The spectacular visual effects of a full-scale film detract from the joint make-believe of living performance in the theatre. Replay facility means that film versions are handy for study, but the references to film in the margins of these revised Notes do not mean that screen is superior to stage. There have been few outstanding film adaptations of Shakespeare, of which perhaps the best have been Olivier's highly theatrical *Henry V* (1944), and Kozintsev's Russian *King Lear* (1964). Yet the cinema is a medium very different to the theatre. An example of what can go wrong with film versions comes in Roman Polanski's 1971 *Macbeth*. As Macbeth begins his soliloquy at II.1.34, 'Is this a dagger which I see before me,/The handle towards my hand?' Polanski has him walking down the castle staircase. At the completion of the first line, a spectral dagger starts into existence and hovers twinkling before Macbeth's eyes. This removes the point that only Macbeth can see the air-borne dagger. He himself says that it may be 'A dagger of the mind, a false creation/ Proceeding from the heat-oppressèd brain,' with 'gouts of blood' on its blade. The audience should collectively imagine it, and realise that Macbeth is the prey to guilty delusions. The film literal-mindedly shows what the audience should imagine.

CRITICAL RECEPTION

There is little criticism of single plays before the 1707 edition of Shakespeare by Nicholas Rowe, a man of the theatre, who wrote of:

> that incomparable character of Shylock the Jew, in *The Merchant of Venice*; but though we have seen that play received and acted as a comedy, and the part of the Jew performed by an excellent comedian, yet I cannot but think it was designed tragically by the author. There appears in it such a deadly spirit of revenge, such a savage fierceness and fellness, and such a bloody designation of cruelty and mischief, as cannot agree either with the style or characters of comedy.

 CHECK THE BOOK
Shakespeare's other Venetian play is *Othello* (1603), the opening of which is also concerned with Venetian justice.

Rowe shows the neoclassical liking of his day for purity of genre. He forgets however that tragedy requires that we should admire the protagonist rather than feel sorry for him. Perhaps Rowe's comments helped to push the 1741 production in a tragic direction. Rowe continued:

The play itself, take it all together, seems to me to be one of the most finished of any of Shakespear's. The tale, indeed, in that part relating to the caskets, and the extravagant and unusual kind of bond given by Antonio, is a little too much removed from the rules of probability: but taking the fact for granted, we must allow it to be very beautifully written. There is something in the friendship of Antonio to Bassanio very great, generous, and tender.

William Hazlitt in his *Characters of Shakespeare's Plays* (1818) wrote:

In proportion as Shylock has ceased to be a popular bugbear, 'baited with the rabble's curse,' he becomes a half-favourite with the philosophical part of the audience, who are disposed to think that Jewish revenge is at least as good as Christian injuries. Shylock is *a good hater*; 'a man no less sinned against than sinning'.

CONTEXT
Jews were allowed to settle in England by Oliver Cromwell in 1655 – so that they should be converted and the Rule of the Saints might begin in England.

Hazlitt added, however, that 'The stage is not in general the best place to study our author's characters in. It is too often filled with traditional commonplace conceptions of the part, handed down from sire to son.' Hazlitt assumes that Shylock is the central figure, reflecting the fact that his passionate speeches tend to dominate the theatre. In the theatre, and in literature since the eighteenth-century's cult of Feeling, intensity of feeling can have more impact than the ethics or conduct of the speaker.

After 1800 the chief change in critical reception, as in theatrical reception, is that Shylock has become not only the focus of interest but the focus of sympathy. Since he was originally, at least to some extent, a comic butt, this unbalances the **comedic** design of the play. Although nineteenth-century critics see that he openly expresses hatred, greed and vengefulness, they are affected by the changing climate of opinion and by the habit, encouraged by Romanticism, of audience-identification with the leading figure in a work of literature or drama. Religious toleration and respect for individual rights were now widespread ideals; Hazlitt's 'philosophical part' of society felt sorry for the oppressed and the excluded. In the twentieth century, notions of European superiority have been shaken, not least by Hitler's policy of genocide against Jews and others. This makes some historical facts a cause for scandal, notably that for centuries a deep distrust of Jews was widespread in England sometimes breaking out in persecution, and ending in the Exclusion of 1290; and others harder to accept, notably the historic Christian doctrines that only Jews who converted could be saved, and that the world could not end until all Jews had been converted.

The critic and the theatre director — especially if Jewish themselves — faced with the historical anti-Semitism of *The Merchant* react in several ways. They can minimise the problem by making the play an unrealistic fairytale or by making Shylock more of a usurer than a Jew. More commonly, they maximise the humanity of Shylock and show anti-Semitism as evil. If as a result the Christians are made not only imperfect but wicked, a worse distortion is created. Although Antonio spits at Shylock, he is ultimately merciful. Some of his young friends prefer golden girls, and others mock Shylock's misfortune. Yet Bassanio remains the hero of the romance (in theatrical terms, the 'young male lead'), and Portia is both the heroine of the romantic comedy and the hero of the trial. One conclusion might be that *The Merchant* is so balanced and interrelated that to maximise or minimise any element, in order to make the play morally consistent or one-sided or unambiguous or politically correct for the twenty-first century, is to reduce its many-sidedness and to iron out its variety of perspectives.

How does this sketch of the course of critical reception help us? It makes us realise that texts change with time and audience. To sum up on Shylock: Shakespeare makes Shylock's Jewishness real to us. Perhaps Shakespeare was dissatisfied with the caricature stage Jew of the flesh-bond story and of Marlowe's *Jew of Malta*. His source-story and his rival's play were intrinsically anti-Semitic, and Shakespeare, however humane, was not above all the prejudices of his time and place. If the story of *The Merchant* is intrinsically anti-Semitic, the play is also *about* anti-Semitism. If Christian mistrust of Jews was racial, religious and commercial, their mistreatment of Jews leads to revenge. Although Shylock's actions are hateful, we can understand some of his feelings. But if Shakespeare considerably humanised his Jew, he still had a flesh-bond story in which the villain is a Jew who prefers his ducats to his daughter, and a pound of flesh to his ducats, and his living to his religion. To say of someone that he wants his pound of flesh is still to say that he wants not merely his full due but the satisfaction of a personal grudge.

QUESTION
The Merchant of Venice has attracted many Jewish critics, directors and actors. Is its final effect anti-Semitic?

CHECK THE BOOK

Diarmaid MacCulloch's *Reformation: Europe's House Divided 1490–1700* (2003) is an informative survey, written very much from a Protestant point of view.

Lastly, however central Shylock has become, Shakespeare interwove the flesh-bond story with the casket story and brought Portia to the rescue. She acts as a kind of providence in his play, preaching a mercy which she later extends to her husband. At the trial's climax she asks a leading question: 'What mercy can you render him, Antonio?' Shakespeare's audience are thus invited to see Antonio's sentence as Christian mercy, exchanging kindness for Shylock's cruelty. What weight should such a strong historical probability have with us? We may think it unfair that Shylock has to become a Christian or die. But we are dealing with Shakespeare's play rather than another play which we might prefer. It belongs then, but it also lives now. It pleases us, but it can still trouble us.

PART FIVE

BACKGROUND

SHAKESPEARE'S LIFE

There are no personal records of Shakespeare's life. Official documents and occasional references to him by contemporary dramatists enable us to draw the main outline of his public life, but his private life remains hidden. Although not at all unusual for a writer of his time, this lack of first-hand evidence has tempted many to read his plays as personal records and to look in them for clues to his character and convictions. The results are unconvincing, partly because Renaissance art was not subjective or designed primarily to express its creator's personality, and partly because the drama of any period is very difficult to read biographically. Except when plays are written by committed dramatists to promote social or political causes (as by Shaw or Brecht), it is all but impossible to decide who amongst the variety of fictional characters in a drama represents the dramatist, or which, if any, of the various and often conflicting points of view expressed is authorial.

What we do know can be quickly summarised. Shakespeare was born into a well-to-do family in the market town of Stratford-upon-Avon in Warwickshire, where he was baptised, in Holy Trinity Church, on 26 April 1564. His father, John Shakespeare, was a prosperous glover and leather merchant who became a person of some importance in the town: in 1565 he was elected an alderman of the town, and in 1568 he became high bailiff (or mayor) of Stratford, though his fortunes soon declined. In 1557 he had married Mary Arden. There is evidence that the family had Catholic sympathies. Their third child (of eight) and eldest son, William, learned to read and write at the primary (or 'petty') school in Stratford and then, it seems highly probable, attended the local grammar school, where he would have studied Latin, history, logic and rhetoric. In November 1582 William, then aged eighteen, married Anne Hathaway, who was twenty-six years old. They had a daughter, Susanna, in May 1583, and twins, Hamnet and Judith, in 1585.

 CHECK THE BOOK
Park Honan's *Shakespeare: A Life*, 1998, is the best recent account. S.Schoenbaum was the leading scholar of the poet's biography and biographers. See his *Shakespeare's Lives*, revised edn., 1991, and other studies.

Shakespeare next appears in the historical record in 1592 when he was mentioned as a London actor and playwright in a pamphlet by the dramatist Robert Greene. These 'lost years' 1585–92 have been the subject of speculation. The most likely theory is that he was a schoolmaster in Lancashire. But we do not know when Shakespeare left Stratford, nor why. In his pamphlet, *Greene's Groatsworth of Wit*, Greene expresses to his fellow dramatists his outrage that the 'upstart crow' Shakespeare has the impudence to believe he 'is as well able to bombast out a blank verse as the best of you'. To have aroused this hostility Shakespeare must, by 1592, have been long enough in London to have made a name for himself as a playwright.

During the next twenty years, Shakespeare continued to live in London, regularly visiting his wife and family in Stratford. He continued to act, but his chief fame was as a dramatist. From 1594 he wrote exclusively for the Lord Chamberlain's Men, which rapidly became the leading dramatic company and from 1603 enjoyed the patronage of James I as the King's Men. His plays were extremely popular and he became a shareholder in his theatre company. He was able to buy lands around Stratford and a large house in the town, to which he retired about 1611. He died there on 23 April 1616 and was buried in Holy Trinity Church on 25 April.

> **CONTEXT**
> The artifice of Elizabethan theatre relied on the audience's active imagination rather than on the 'willing suspension of disbelief' proposed in the Shakespearean criticism of the Romantic critic S. T. Coleridge.

HIS DRAMATIC CAREER

Between the late 1580s and 1613 Shakespeare wrote thirty-seven plays, and contributed to some by other dramatists. This was by no means an exceptional number for a professional playwright of the times. The exact date of the composition of individual plays is a matter of debate – for only a few plays is the date of their first performance known – but the broad outlines of Shakespeare's dramatic career have been established. He began in the late 1580s and early 1590s by rewriting earlier plays and working with plotlines inspired by the Classics. He concentrated on comedies (such as *The Comedy of Errors*, 1590–4, which derived from the Latin playwright Plautus) and plays dealing with English history (such as the three parts of *Henry VI*, 1589–92), though he also tried his hand at bloodthirsty revenge tragedy (*Titus Andronicus*, 1592–3, indebted to both Ovid and Seneca). During the 1590s Shakespeare developed his expertise in these kinds of play to write such comic masterpieces such as *A Midsummer Night's Dream* (1594–5) and *As*

You Like It (1599–1600) and history plays such as *Henry IV* (1596–8) and *Henry V* (1598–9).

As the new century begins a new note is detectable. Plays such as *Troilus and Cressida* (1601–2) and *Measure for Measure* (1603–4), poised between comedy and tragedy, evoke complex responses. Because of their generic uncertainty and ambivalent tone such works are sometimes referred to as 'problem plays', but it is tragedy which comes to dominate the extraordinary sequence of masterpieces: *Hamlet* (1600–1), *Othello* (1602–4), *King Lear* (1605–6), *Macbeth* (1605–6) and *Antony and Cleopatra* (1606).

In the last years of his dramatic career, Shakespeare wrote a group of plays of a quite different kind. These 'romances', as they are often called, are in many ways the most remarkable of all his plays. The group comprises *Pericles* (1608), *Cymbeline* (1609–11), *The Winter's Tale* (1610–11) and *The Tempest* (1610–11). These plays (particularly *Cymbeline*) take up many of the situations and themes of the earlier dramas but in fantastical and exotic dramatic designs which, set in distant lands, covering large tracts of time and involving music, mime, dance and tableaux, have something of the qualities of masques and pageants. The situations which in the tragedies had led to disaster are here resolved: the great theme is restoration and reconciliation. Where in the tragedies Ophelia, Desdemona and Cordelia died, the daughters of these plays – Marina, Imogen, Perdita, Miranda – survive and are reunited with their parents and lovers.

THE TEXTS OF SHAKESPEARE'S PLAYS

Nineteen of Shakespeare's plays were printed during his lifetime in what are called 'quartos' (books, each containing one play, and made up of sheets of paper each folded twice to make four leaves). Shakespeare, however, did not supervise the publication of these plays. This was not unusual. When a playwright had sold a play to a dramatic company he sold his rights in it: copyright belonged to whoever had possession of an actual copy of the text, and so consequently authors had no control over what happened their work. Anyone who could get hold of the text of a play might publish it if they wished. Hence, what found its way into print might be the author's copy, but it might be an actor's copy or a

> **CONTEXT**
>
> Plays were not considered as serious literature in this period: when in 1612, Sir Thomas Bodley was setting up his library in Oxford he instructed his staff not to buy any drama for the collection: 'haply [perhaps] some plays may be worthy the keeping, but hardly one in forty.'

The Text of Shakespeare's Plays continued

prompt copy, perhaps cut or altered for performance; sometimes, actors (or even members of the audience) might publish what they could remember of the text. Printers, working without the benefit of the author's oversight, introduced their own errors, through misreading the manuscript for example, and by 'correcting' what seemed to them not to make sense.

> **CONTEXT**
>
> Portia's miraculous rescue of Antonio is an example of *deus ex machina* of classical drama: the lowering by mechanical means onto the stage of a god(dess) who brings order out of chaos.

In 1623 John Heminges and Henry Condell, two actors in Shakespeare's company, collected together texts of thirty-six of Shakespeare's plays (*Pericles* was omitted) and published them in a large folio (a book in which each sheet of paper is folded once in half, to give two leaves). This, the First Folio, was followed by later editions in 1632, 1663 and 1685. Despite its appearance of authority, however, the texts in the First Folio still present many difficulties, for there are printing errors and confused passages in the plays, and its texts can differ significantly from those of the earlier quartos, when these exist.

Shakespeare's texts have, then, been through a number of inter-mediaries. We do not have his authority for any one of his plays, and hence we cannot be certain exactly what it was that he wrote. Bibliographers, textual critics and editors have spent a great deal of effort on trying to get behind the errors, uncertainties and contradictions in the available texts to recover the plays as Shakespeare originally wrote them. What we read is the result of these efforts. Modern texts are what editors have constructed from the available evidence: they do not correspond exactly to any sixteenth- or seventeenth-century editions, nor to the text of an early performance of a Shakespeare play. Furthermore, these composite texts differ from each other, for different editors read the early texts differently and in some places come to different conclusions. A Shakespeare text is the product of a lot of editorial work.

Often, of course, its judgements embody, if not the personal prejudices of the editor, then the cultural preferences of the time in which he or she was working. Growing awareness of this has led some recent scholars to become sceptical about the idea of a 'perfect' text. Stanley Wells and Gary Taylor, the editors of the Oxford edition of *The Complete Works* (1988), point out that almost certainly the texts of Shakespeare's plays were altered in performance, and from one performance to another, so that there may never have been a single, correct and final version. They note, too, that Shakespeare probably revised and rewrote some plays. They do not claim to print a definitive text of any play, but prefer what seems to them the 'more theatrical' version; and in one instance, when there is a great difference between available versions, as with *King Lear*, they print two texts.

SHAKESPEARE AND THE ENGLISH RENAISSANCE

Shakespeare arrived in London at the very time that the Elizabethan period produced what was later called a 'golden age' of English literature. Although Elizabeth reigned as queen from 1558 to 1603, the term 'Elizabethan' can be used very loosely, in literary parlance, to refer to the period 1580 to 1625, when the great works of the age were produced. (The later part of this period is properly called 'Jacobean', from 'Jacobus', the Latin form of the name of the king who succeeded Elizabeth, James I of England and VI of Scotland, who reigned from 1603 to 1625.) The poet Edmund Spenser heralded this literary period with his pastoral poem *The Shepheardes Calender* (1579). In his essay *An Apologie for Poetrie* (written about 1580, although not published until 1595), Sir Philip Sidney championed the imaginative power of the 'speaking picture of poesy', famously declaring that 'Nature never set forth the earth in so rich a tapestry as divers poets have done. ... Her world is brazen, the poets only deliver a golden'.

CHECK THE NET

An online text of the Geneva Bible is available at http://www.geneva bible.org/

Spenser and Sidney were part of that rejuvenating movement in European culture which since the nineteenth century has been known by the term *Renaissance*. Meaning literally *rebirth* it denotes a revival and redirection of artistic and intellectual endeavour which began in Italy in the fourteenth century in the poetry of Petrarch. It spread gradually northwards across Europe, and is detectable in England in the early sixteenth century in the writings of the scholar and statesman Sir Thomas More and in the poetry of Sir Thomas Wyatt and Henry Howard, Earl of Surrey. Its keynote was a curiosity in thought which challenged old assumptions and traditions, together with some high hopes for secular literature.

That spirit was fuelled by the rediscovery of many Classical texts and the culture of Greece and Rome. This fostered a confidence in human reason and in human potential which, in every sphere, challenged old convictions. The discovery of America and its peoples (Columbus had sailed in 1492) demonstrated that the world was a larger and stranger place than had been thought. The cosmological speculation of Copernicus (later confirmed by Galileo) that the sun, not the earth was the centre of our planetary system challenged the ancient belief that the earth and human beings were at the centre of the cosmos. The pragmatic political philosophy of Machiavelli seemed to cut politics free from its traditional link with morality by appearing to permit to statesmen any means which secured the desired end. And in some northern countries the religious movements we know collectively as the Reformation broke with the Church of Rome and set the individual conscience, not ecclesiastical authority, at the centre of the religious life, although the state church punished those who did not conform to the state religion. Nothing, it seemed, was beyond questioning, everything might be changed.

Shakespeare's drama is innovative and challenging in the way of the Renaissance. It questions the beliefs, assumptions and politics upon which Elizabethan society was founded. And although the plays always conclude in a restoration of order and stability, and none can be read as justifying regicide, many recent critics argue that their imaginative energy goes into questioning, rather than reinforcing, traditional values. They point out that the famous speech on hierarchical order in *Troilus and Cressida* (I.3.86–124) or Katerina's speech on wifely submission to patriarchal authority in *The Taming of the Shrew* (V.2.146–60) appear to be rendered **ironic** by the action of the plays in which they occur. Convention, audience expectation and censorship all required the *status quo* to be endorsed by the plots' conclusions, but the dramas find ways to allow alternative sentiments to be expressed. Frequently, figures of authority are undercut by some **comic** or **parodic** figure: against the Duke in *Measure for Measure* is set Lucio; against Prospero in *The Tempest*, Caliban; against Henry IV, Falstaff. Despairing, critical, dissident, disillusioned, unbalanced, rebellious, mocking voices can be heard in the plays, rejecting, resenting, defying the established order. They often belong to marginal, socially unacceptable figures, 'licensed', as

CHECK THE BOOK

A useful corrective to Anglican views of the English Reformation is Eamon Duffy's *The Stripping of the Altars*, 1992

it were, by their situations to say what would be unacceptable from socially privileged or responsible citizens. Are such characters given these views to discredit them, or were they the only ones through whom a voice could be given to radical and dissident ideas? To what extent might Shylock be such a figure?

Renaissance culture was often nationalistic. With the break-up of the internationalism of the Middle Ages the evolving nation states which still mark the map of Europe began for the first time to acquire distinctive cultural identities. There was intense rivalry among them as they sought to achieve in their own vernacular languages a culture which could equal that of Greece and Rome. Spenser's great allegorical epic poem *The Faerie Queene*, which began to appear from 1590, celebrated Elizabeth and was intended to outdo the poetic achievements of Italy, Spain and France and to stand beside works of Virgil and Homer. Shakespeare, too, is concerned with national identity. His history plays tell an epic story which examines how modern England came into being through the conflicts of the fifteenth-century Wars of the Roses which brought the Tudors to the throne. He is fascinated, too, by the related subject of politics and the exercise of power. With the collapse of medieval feudalism and the authority of local barons, the royal court in the Renaissance came to assume a new status as the centre of power and patronage. It was here that the destiny of a country was shaped. Courts, and how to succeed in them, consequently fascinated the Renaissance; and they fascinated Shakespeare and his audience.

CHECK THE BOOK
Michael Mangan, *A Preface to Shakespeare's Comedies*, 1996, is lively and accessible.

That is why we are usually at court in his plays, and in the company of courtiers. But the dramatic gaze is not merely admiring; through a variety of devices, a critical perspective is brought to bear. The court may be paralleled by a very different world, revealing comical similarities (for example, Henry's court and the Boar's Head tavern, ruled over by Falstaff in *Henry IV*). Its hypocrisy may be bitterly denounced (for example, in the diatribes of the mad Lear) and its self-seeking ambition represented disturbingly in the figure of a Machiavellian villain (such as Edmund in *Lear*) or a malcontent (such as Iago in *Othello*). Shakespeare is fond of displacing the court to another context, the better to examine its assumptions and pretensions and to offer alternatives to the courtly life (for example, in the pastoral setting of the forest of Arden in *As You Like It* or

Prospero's island in *The Tempest*). Courtiers are frequently figures of fun whose unmanly sophistication ('neat and trimly dressed, / Fresh as a bridegroom ... perfumed like a milliner', says Hotspur of such a man in *Henry IV*, I.3.33–6) is contrasted with plain-speaking integrity: Oswald is set against Kent in *King Lear*.

(When thinking of these matters, we should remember that stage plays were subject to censorship, and any criticism had therefore to be muted or oblique: direct criticism of the monarch or the contemporary English court would not be tolerated. This has something to do with why the plays are set either in the past, or abroad.)

The nationalism of the English Renaissance was reinforced by Protestantism. Henry VIII had broken with Rome in the 1530s and Queen Elizabeth established a Protestant state church. Because the Pope had excommunicated Elizabeth as a heretic and relieved the English of their allegiance to the Crown, there was government suspicion of Roman Catholics as potential traitors. There was persecution of Catholics in Warwickshire. The Spanish Armada of 1588 was a crusade to restore England to Roman Catholic allegiance; Catholicism was hence easily associated with disloyalty and treachery. Shakespeare's plays, although generally Christian and even at times sacramental, are remarkably free from sectarian sentiment, although Puritans, extreme Protestants, are portrayed as ridiculous: for example, Malvolio in *Twelfth Night*.

CHECK THE BOOK

The standard scholarly book on the theatre at this time is Andrew Gurr's *The Shakespearean Stage* (1992).

The central figures of the plays are frequently individuals beset by temptation, by the lure of evil – Angelo in *Measure for Measure*, Othello, Lear, Macbeth. We follow their inner struggles. Shakespeare's protagonists have the preoccupation with self and the introspective tendencies encouraged by Protestantism: his tragic heroes are haunted by their consciences, seeking their true selves, agonising over what course of action to take as they follow what can often be understood as a kind of spiritual progress towards heaven, purgatory or hell.

SHAKESPEARE'S THEATRE

The theatre for which the plays were written was one of the most remarkable innovations of the Renaissance. Although religious and civic drama had flourished since the fourteenth century, and continued until Shakespeare's childhood, there had been no theatres in the medieval period. Performed in churches, on carts and in open spaces at Christian festivals, plays had been almost exclusively religious. Some professional actors wandered the country putting on entertainments in the yards of inns, on makeshift stages in market squares, or anywhere else suitable. They did not perform full-length plays, but mimes, juggling and comedy acts. Such actors were regarded by officialdom as little better than vagabonds.

Just before Shakespeare went to London all this began to change. A number of young men who had been to the universities of Oxford and Cambridge came to London in the 1580s and began to write plays which made use of what they had learned about the Classical drama of ancient Greece and Rome. Plays such as John Lyly's *Alexander and Campaspe* (1584), Christopher Marlowe's *Tamburlaine the Great* (about 1587) and Thomas Kyd's *The Spanish Tragedy* (1588–9) were unlike anything that had been written in English before. They were full-length plays on secular subjects, taking their plots from history and legend, adopting many of the devices of Classical drama, and offering a range of characterisation and situation hitherto unattempted in English drama. With the exception of Lyly's prose dramas, they were in the unrhymed iambic pentameters (blank verse) which the Earl of Surrey had introduced into English earlier in the sixteenth century. This was a freer and more expressive medium than the rhymed verse of medieval drama. It was the drama of these 'university wits' which Shakespeare —not a university man— challenged when he came to London. Greene was one of them, and we have heard how little he liked this Shakespeare setting himself up as a dramatist.

The most significant change of all, however, was that these dramatists wrote for the professional theatre. In 1576 James Burbage built the first permanent theatre in England, in Shoreditch,

> **CONTEXT**
>
> The culture of the Elizabethans was less visual than ours, more oral and aural. Listening to sermons was popular. We speak of going to see a play, but Elizabethans would 'go to hear a play', as in the Induction to *The Taming of the Shrew*, 2.130.

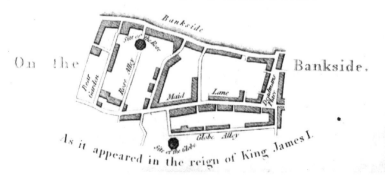

THE GLOBE THEATRE,

On the Bankside.

As it appeared in the reign of King James I.

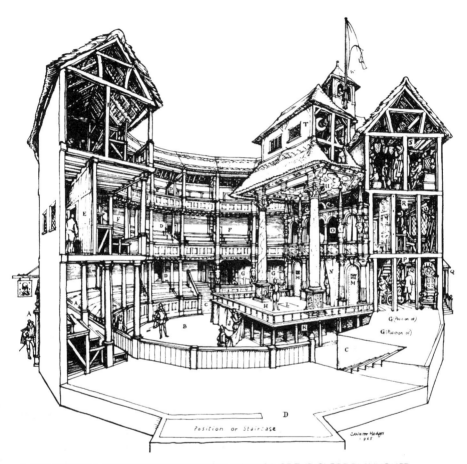

A CONJECTURAL RECONSTRUCTION OF THE INTERIOR OF THE GLOBE PLAYHOUSE

AA	Main entrance
B	The Yard
CC	Entrances to lowest galleries
D	Entrance to staircase and upper galleries
E	Corridor serving the different sections of the middle gallery
F	Middle gallery ('Twopenny Rooms')
G	'Gentlemen's Rooms or Lords Rooms'
H	The stage
J	The hanging being put up round the stage
K	The 'Hell' under the stage
L	The stage trap, leading down to the Hell
MM	Stage doors
N	Curtained 'place behind the stage'
O	Gallery above the stage, used as required sometimes by musicians, sometimes by spectators, and often as part of the play
P	Back-stage area (the tiring-house)
Q	Tiring-house door
R	Dressing-rooms
S	Wardrobe and storage
T	The hut housing the machine for lowering enthroned gods, etc., to the stage
U	The 'Heavens'
W	Hoisting the playhouse flag

just beyond London's northern boundary. It was called simply 'The Theatre'. Others soon followed. Thus, when Shakespeare came to London, there was a flourishing drama, theatres and companies of actors waiting for him, such as there had never been before in England. His company performed at James Burbage's Theatre until 1596, and used the Swan and Curtain until they moved into their own new theatre, The Globe, in 1599. It was burned down in 1613 when a cannon was fired during a performance of Shakespeare's *Henry VIII*.

> **CONTEXT**
>
> Shakespeare's acting company would not have had personal copies of the playscript. Instead, they would only have been given their own lines to learn.

With the completion in 1996 of Sam Wanamaker's project to construct in London a replica of The Globe, and with productions now running there, a version of Shakespeare's theatre can be experienced at first-hand. It is very different to the usual modern experience of drama. The form of the Elizabethan theatre derived from the inn yards and animal-baiting rings in which actors had been accustomed to perform in the past. They were circular wooden buildings with a paved courtyard in the middle open to the sky. A rectangular stage jutted out into the middle of this yard. Much of the audience stood in the yard (or 'pit') to watch the play. They were thus on three sides of the stage, close up to it and on a level with it. These 'groundlings' paid only a penny to get in, but for wealthier spectators there were seats in three covered tiers or galleries between the inner and outer walls of the building, extending round most of the auditorium and overlooking the pit and the stage. Such a theatre could hold about 3,000 spectators. The yards were just over 24 metres in diameter and the rectangular stage approximately 12 metres by 9 metres and 1.67 metres high. Shakespeare aptly called such a theatre a 'wooden O' in the Prologue to *Henry V* (line 13).

The stage itself was partially covered by a roof or canopy which projected from the wall at the rear of the stage and was supported by two posts at the front. This protected the stage and performers from inclement weather, and to it were secured winches and other machinery for stage effects. On either side at the back of the stage was a door. These led into the dressing room (or 'tiring house') and it was by means of these doors that actors entered and left the stage. Between these doors was a small recess or alcove which was curtained off. Such a 'discovery place' served, for example, for

Juliet's bedroom when in Act IV Scene 4 of *Romeo and Juliet* the Nurse went to the back of the stage and drew the curtain to find, or in Elizabethan English 'discover', Juliet apparently dead on her bed. Above the discovery place was a balcony, used for the famous balcony scenes of *Romeo and Juliet* (II.2 and III.5), and for Jessica to throw the casket from in *The Merchant*. Actors (all parts in the Elizabethan theatre were taken by boys or men) had access to the area beneath the stage; from here, in the 'cellarage', would have come the voice of the ghost of Hamlet's father (*Hamlet*, II.1.150–82).

On these stages there was very little in the way of scenery or props – there was nowhere to store them (there were no wings in this theatre) nor any way to set them up (no tabs across the stage), and, anyway, productions had to be transportable for performance at court or at noble houses. The stage was bare, which is why characters often tell us where they are: there was nothing on the stage to indicate location. It is also why location is rarely topographical, and more often symbolic. It suggests a dramatic mood or situation, rather than a place: Lear's barren heath reflects his destitute state, as the storm his emotional turmoil. 'Belmont' means 'beautiful hill'.

None of the plays printed in Shakespeare's lifetime marks Act or scene divisions. These have been introduced by later editors, but they should not mislead us into supposing that there was any break in Elizabethan performances such as might happen today while the curtains are closed and the set is changed. The staging of Elizabethan plays was continuous, with the many short 'scenes' of which Shakespeare's plays are often constructed following one after another in quick succession. We have to think of a more fluid and much faster production than we are generally used to: in the prologues to *Romeo and Juliet* (line 12) and *Henry VIII* (line 13) Shakespeare speaks of only two hours as the playing time. It is because plays were staged continuously that exits and entrances are written in as part of the script: characters speak as they enter or leave the stage because otherwise there would be a silence while, in full view, they took up their positions. (This is also why dead bodies are carried off: they cannot get up and walk off.)

In 1608, Shakespeare's company, the King's Men, acquired the Blackfriars Theatre, a smaller, rectangular indoor theatre, holding

> **? QUESTION**
> If you were a director, where would you place the interval in *The Merchant of Venice*?

CHECK THE BOOK

The Literary Language of Shakespeare, by S.S.Hussey, 1982, shows how the arts of composing in verse and in prose were studied according to the rules of the ancient art of rhetoric.

about 700 people, with seats for all the members of the audience, facilities for elaborate stage effects and, because it was enclosed, artificial lighting. It has been suggested that the plays written for this 'private' theatre differed from those written for The Globe, since, as it cost more to go to a private theatre, the audience came from a higher social stratum and demanded the more elaborate and courtly entertainment which Shakespeare's romances provide. However, the King's Men continued to play in The Globe in the summer, using Blackfriars in the winter, and it is not certain that Shakespeare's last plays were written specifically for the Blackfriars Theatre, or first performed there.

READING SHAKESPEARE

Shakespeare's plays were written for this stage, but it can almost be said that they were written *by* this stage. The material and physical circumstances of their production in such theatres had a profound effect upon the nature of Elizabethan plays. Unless we bear this in mind, we are likely to find them very strange, for we will read with expectations shaped by our own familiarity with modern fiction and modern drama. This is, by and large, realistic; it seeks to persuade us that what we are reading or watching is really happening. This is quite foreign to Shakespeare. If we try to read him like this, we shall find ourselves irritated by the improbabilities of his plot, confused by his chronology, puzzled by locations, frustrated by unanswered questions and dissatisfied by the motivation of the action. The absurd ease with which disguised persons pass through Shakespeare's plays is a case in point: why does no-one recognise people they know so well? There is a great deal of psychological accuracy in Shakespeare's plays, but we are far from any attempt at realism.

The reason is that in Shakespeare's theatre it was impossible to pretend that the audience was not watching a contrived performance. In a modern theatre, the audience is encouraged to forget itself as it becomes absorbed by the action on stage. The worlds of the spectators and of the actors are sharply distinguished by the lighting: in the dark auditorium the audience is passive, silent, anonymous, receptive and attentive; on the lighted stage the actors are active, vocal, demonstrative and dramatic. (The distinction is still more marked in the cinema.) There is no communication between the two worlds: for the audience to speak would be to interrupt; for the actors to address the audience would be to break the illusion of the play. In the Elizabethan theatre, this distinction did not exist, and for two reasons: first, performances took place in the open air and in daylight which illuminated everyone; secondly, the spectators were all around the stage (wealthier spectators could be on it), and were dressed no differently to the actors, who wore contemporary dress. In such a theatre, spectators would be as aware of each other as of the actors; they could not lose their identity in a corporate group, nor could they ever forget that they were spectators at a performance. There was no chance that they could believe 'this is really happening'.

This, then, was communal theatre, not only in the sense that it was going on in the middle of a crowd but in the sense that the crowd joined in. Elizabethan audiences had little deference: they did not keep quiet, or arrive on time, or remain for the whole performance. They joined in, interrupted, even getting on the stage. And plays were preceded and followed by jigs and clowning. It was all much more like our experience of a pantomime, and at a pantomime we are fully aware, and are meant to be aware, that we are watching games being played with reality. The conventions of pantomime revel in their own artificiality: the fishnet tights are to signal that the handsome prince is a woman, the Dame's large false breasts signal that 'she' is a man.

Something very similar is the case with Elizabethan theatre: it utilised its very theatricality. Instead of trying to persuade spectators that they are not in a theatre watching a performance, Elizabethan plays acknowledge the audience. It is addressed not only by prologues, epilogues and choruses, but in soliloquies. There is no realistic reason why characters should suddenly explain themselves to empty rooms, but, of course, it is not an empty room. The actor is surrounded by people. Soliloquies are not addressed to the world of the play: they are for the audience's benefit. And that audience's complicity is assumed: when a character like Prospero declares himself to be invisible, it is accepted that he is. Disguises are taken to be impenetrable, however improbable, and we are to accept impossibly contrived situations, such as barely hidden characters remaining undetected (indeed, on the Elizabethan stage there was nowhere they could hide).

> **CONTEXT**
>
> The Globe could take 3,000 spectators, and there were several other theatres. As there were about 200,000 Londoners, a lot of them could go to the theatre in one day.

These, then, are plays which are aware of themselves as dramas; in critical terminology, they are self-reflexive, commenting upon themselves as dramatic pieces and prompting the audience to think about the theatrical experience. They do this not only through their direct address to the audience but through their fondness for the play-within-a-play and their constant use of images from, and allusions to, the theatre. They are fascinated by role playing, by acting, appearance and reality. Things are rarely what they seem, either in comedy (for example, in *A Midsummer Night's Dream*) or tragedy (*Romeo and Juliet*). This offers one way to think about those disguises: they are thematic rather than realistic. Kent's disguise in *Lear* reveals his true, loyal self, while Edmund, who is not disguised, hides his true self. In *As You Like It*, Rosalind is more truly her female self when disguised as a man than when dressed as a woman. This is not so true of Portia.

> **CONTEXT**
>
> The poet Walter Raleigh wrote a poem on this image of life as theatre, which begins 'What is our life? A play of passion' in which 'our mothers' wombs the tiring houses be/when we are dressed for this short comedy'. There is a twist at the end of the short verse: 'only we die in earnest that's no jest'.

The effect of all this is to confuse the distinction we would make between 'real life' and 'acting'. The case of Rosalind, for example, raises searching questions about gender roles, about how far it is 'natural' to be womanly or manly: how does the stage, on which a man can play a woman playing a man (and have a man fall in love with him/her), differ from life, in which we assume the roles we think appropriate to masculine and feminine behaviour? The same is true of political roles: when a Richard II or Lear is so aware of the regal part he is performing, of the trappings and rituals of kingship, their plays raise the uncomfortable possibility that the answer to the question, what constitutes a successful king, is simply: a good actor. Indeed, human life generally is repeatedly rendered through the imagery of the stage, from Macbeth's 'Life's but a walking shadow, a poor player / That struts and frets his hour upon the stage / And then is heard no more ...' (V.5.23–5) to Prospero's paralleling of human life to a performance which, like the globe (both world and theatre) will end (IV.1.146–58). When life is a fiction, like this play, or this play is a fiction like life, what is the difference? 'All the world's a stage ...' (*As You Like It*, II.7.139).

In such a theatre, the playwright's prime means to make the audience imagine and believe more than they could physically see was his use of language.

LITERARY BACKGROUND

SOURCES

Shakespeare made the story of his play by combining elements from several sources and analogues, changing and adding important details of his own:

CHECK THE BOOK
One source for Shylock was Barabas in Christopher Marlowe's *The Jew of Malta*.

1 A lost play called *The Jew* (*c*.1578), reported by Stephen Gosson to represent 'the greediness of worldly choosers, and bloody minds of usurers'.

2 The story of Giannetto in *Il Pecorone* (The Muttonhead), a collection of fifty tales modelled on the *Decameron* of Boccaccio, by a fourteenth-century contemporary of Geoffrey Chaucer, Ser Giovanni of Florence, printed in 1558 in Italian. This has two Venetian friends, a loan, a Lady of Belmonte, a flesh-bond with a Jew, the Lady disguised as lawyer, a trial which turns upon taking exactly one pound of flesh without a drop of blood, a bridal ring trick, and a final marriage.

3 Christopher Marlowe's *The Jew of Malta* (*c*.1589): the protagonist Barabas is a forcefully ingenious trickster-villain, who blows up a convent of nuns in which his daughter Abigail (who loves a Christian) has taken refuge. The father-daughter relationship is a parallel with that of Shylock and Jessica. The wicked Barabas is more enjoyable than his Christian opponents.

4 The thirty-second History of the medieval *Gesta Romanorum* has a choice of caskets leading to marriage, with many similarities to Shakespeare's; but the chooser is a woman.

5 The fourteenth story of Masuccio's *Il Novellino* (1476): a miser's daughter elopes, taking his money with her (like Jessica; but neither is Jewish).

6 Anthony Munday's prose tale *Zelauto* (1580) has two lovers, a money-lender, a flesh-bond, two ladies dressed up as lawyers, no drop of blood to be shed, a double wedding.

CHECK THE BOOK

The annual *Shakespeare Survey* is a source of up to date scholarship and criticism. A good historical article is Philip Brockbank's 'Shakespeare and the Fashion of These Times', vol, 16, 1963.

7 A ballad of *Gernutus*, a Jew foiled of his bond, of roughly the same time as *The Merchant*.

8 Alexandre Silvain's *The Orator*, translated from the French, probably by Munday (see 6 above), 1596. His Declamation 95, 'Of a Jew, who would for his debt have a pound of flesh of a Christian' has arguments similar to those used in the Trial Scene.

Of these, 2 and 3 are most important, followed by 4, 6 and 8. In *Il Pecorone*, Giannetto is the adopted son (not the younger friend) of a wealthy Venetian, Ansaldo. The Lady of Belmonte wants Giannetto to sleep with her but drugs his drink: his ship is forfeit. She tries him again and he fails again. At the third attempt, a servant-girl warns Giannetto about the drink; this time he succeeds in sleeping with the Lady. Ansaldo had financed the first two expeditions but borrows money from a Jew for the third. The forfeit is a pound of flesh, but the disguised Lady/lawyer foils the wicked Jew and plays the ring-trick on Giannetto. Ansaldo marries the servant-girl. The similarities are striking, but so are Shakespeare's changes (his Lady is ideally virtuous), and his additions: the caskets, the elopement of Jessica, the doubling of the ring-trick, and much else. The Italian source is comic, thin and crude in comparison.

Shakespeare liked to find his ingredients in existing stories, and to combine, change and transform, inventing only when he had to. He enriched what he took with new motifs, ideas and feelings, producing complexity of theme. By this stage in his career, his resources of mind, verse and language give his plays an orchestral quality, with theme and motif echoed everywhere.

Il Pecorone is a prose tale, but Marlowe's *Jew of Malta* is a play and a masterpiece. The original and forceful Marlowe dominated the London stage for ten years; he was killed in 1594. Shakespeare's *Richard II*, composed at much the same time as his *Merchant*, owes much to Marlowe's *Edward II*. Shakespeare admired and learned from Marlowe, but he had a very different kind of mind, and did not merely copy. Marlowe's play concerns a Jew and his daughter who loves a Christian; and pits Jew against Christian. But *The Jew of Malta* mixes tragic farce and heartless comedy with cynical satire on the greed of Christian, Turk and Jew. Barabas is a comic villain superior in intelligence to Christian and Turk. Marlowe's play thus lacks romance, poetry and any interest in loving and giving. Yet its Barabas is wonderfully compelling.

HISTORICAL BACKGROUND

JEWS AND CHRISTIANS

The Jews are God's chosen people, according to the book of Genesis, the first book in the Hebrew Scriptures, the Old Testament of the Christian Bible. Christians believe that the Saviour or Messiah looked forward to by the Jewish prophets in the Old Testament is Jesus, the Christ, and that he is the Son of God. The New Testament of the Bible reports that Jesus was rejected and crucified at the insistence of the Jewish mob: 'Then answered all the people, and said, His blood be on us, and on our children' (Matthew 27:25). The destruction of Jerusalem by the Romans in AD70 was interpreted by medieval Christians as retribution for the killing of the Messiah. From that period, Jews left Israel in the Diaspora (Scattering) and spread over the Old World, living in cities in separate communities distinguished by religion, by ritual, hygiene and diet, and by dress. Judaism kept Jews ethnically distinct, for a Jew is the child of a Jewish mother: marrying a non-Jew is forbidden, and Jews do not seek converts. One usually becomes a Jew by birth or by marrying a Jew and converting, whereas Christianity is international and non-racial. As aliens and non-citizens, medieval Jews could not own land, and often worked as jewellers and moneylenders (an unpopular profession); a few became rich. Jews lent money to the King; they thus provided a useful but disreputable service. Christians believed (though 'baptism by desire' now liberally extends this proviso) that salvation is only by baptism, and that Jews cannot be saved except by Christian conversion and baptism. Yet the Jews, the Chosen People, are not like other non-Christians, and it is part of Christian tradition that the world will not end until the conversion of the Jews.

USURY

In the Old Testament, the exacting of interest on a loan was forbidden to Jews who were lending to Jews. In the Middle Ages it was forbidden to Christian clerics, and then to laymen, although in 1215 a Council of the Church allowed Jews to take interest. In

 CHECK THE BOOK
Shakespeare Quarterly is worth consulting for recent scholarship. Still valuable is J.W.Lever, 'Shylock, Portia and the Values of Shakespearean Comedy ', 3, 1952.

medieval theory, money was a medium of exchange, not a commodity in itself. Aristotle had taught that money could not breed money: it was 'barren' (Antonio's argument in Act I Scene 3). After the rise of capitalism, the sixteenth-century reformers relaxed this teaching; Calvin permitted the taking of interest, and in England in 1571 moderate interest was no longer prohibited by civil law. In the 1650s Oliver Cromwell permitted Jews to return to England. In Catholic countries toleration of usury came late; not in France until 1789. Islam still forbids usury. Shylock is a usurer, whereas Antonio is a merchant venturer, a new and glamorous occupation in Elizabethan England. We know that Shakespeare, a financial partner in his own theatre company, also invested in the Company which developed Virginia. Today, the most lucrative form of capitalism is trading in money itself.

> **CONTEXT**
>
> *The Merchant of Venice* can be compared with *Measure for Measure* (1604) as a comedy dealing with intractable problems of justice and mercy.

The practice of giving credit and charging interest, the basis of modern banking, developed in the trading cities of Europe after AD1100, especially in the cities of Lombardy in northern Italy (hence Lombard St, a bankers' street in the City of London). Jewish lenders were dependent on royal favour, and kings sometimes repudiated their debts to Jews.

ANTI-SEMITISM

In 1290 King Edward I banished Jews from England. Thereafter they did not live openly in England; a few stayed on, converting or apparently conforming to Christianity. English people knew Jews only from legend. In the popular medieval Mystery Plays, which lasted until Shakespeare's youth, Jews featured as a cursed race. It was rumoured that they killed children and drank their blood. In the legend of Little St Hugh of Lincoln (d. 1255), retold in Chaucer's Prioress's Tale, Jews murder a Christian child.

An association with anti-Semitic legends of ritual sacrifice is half-suggested in the trial scene by Shylock's knife. The Jewish Paschal feast involves the sacrifice of a lamb, whereas in Christian belief Christ at his last Paschal supper instituted the Eucharist as an unbloody sacrifice. Christians see Christ as the final sacrificial scapegoat.

Despite what popular Christianity may have thought, Judaism has always been against human sacrifice. God made it clear to the patriarch Abraham that he demanded obedience not sacrifice: once Abraham had shown willingness to sacrifice Isaac, God provided a ram to sacrifice instead (Genesis 24–28). Animal sacrifice was later regarded by Jewish spiritual writers as an external if necessary observance. But the Gospels begin with Herod's massacre of the innocents (Jews killing children), and end with the Crucifixion. In the Gospel account of this, in response to the Roman Governor Pilate saying 'I am innocent of the blood of this just man: see ye to it', there follows a verse in which the Jews take responsibility for the death of Jesus: 'Then answered all the people, and said, His blood be upon us and upon our children' (Matthew, Chapter 27, Verse 2). Jesus later forgave his killers, saying 'they know not what they do' (Luke 23: 34). Orthodox Christianity has often declared that it does not hold the Jewish people responsible for the death of Christ. Yet popular Christianity has sometimes recalled that the Jewish people took the blame upon themselves and their children, and has quoted this ancestral curse as a pretext for treating the Jews as scapegoats for all sorts of ills.

St Paul, a Jew, encouraged Christians to regard Judaism as bound by the Old Law of justice, and themselves, whether Jewish or Gentile, as bound by the New Law of love. This bears on the contest of justice and mercy, retaliation and forgiveness, a theme of the play (see Themes). Despite these entrenched prejudices, stage Jews could also become caricature figures of fun and fantastic mischief as well as of hostility, as in Marlowe's Barabas.

Anti-Semitism has often been regarded as sinful, since Christianity developed out of Judaism. Semites are the sons of Shem, one of Noah's three sons, from whom humanity descends. In biblical tradition, the inhabitants of the region of Palestine, Arab as well as Jew, descend from Shem. Despite its etymology, 'anti-Semitism' means prejudice against Jews rather than against Levantines in general. And despite official Christian teaching, European history has been disfigured by discrimination against Jews. Jews were tolerated in England in the later seventeenth century, and allowed to work in the City of London. This gradually affected the reception of *The Merchant of Venice*. A new phase was opened in 1945, when the full horrors of the Nazi genocide of Jews became undeniable public knowledge (see **Critical history**). Judaism is a racial religion, in that

CHECK THE FILM
The best film versions of *The Merchant of Venice* are probably those by Jonathan Miller, and that of the Royal National Theatre, Directed by Trevor Nunn, 2000, with Henry Goodman as Shylock, RSC Video 60004, DVD 63034. Try to see two versions.

only those who are Jewish by birth or marry a Jew can be admitted to Judaism. A xenophobic anti-Semitism has often been experienced by Jews, whether they practise their religion or not, and not only in Christian or Muslim countries. Nazism was un-Christian, and its anti-Semitism was based not on religion but on race. From the Roman destruction of Jerusalem in the year 70 until the twentieth century, virtually all Jews lived outside Israel. Having no land of their own, they were outsiders and liable to local resentment, especially at a crisis. The creation of the modern state of Israel, opposed by Arab and other Muslims, and the fact that most of the Jews in the world now live in its most powerful country, the United States, has further altered, and internationalised, the reception of this play.

VENICE

Venice was a city which fascinated the Elizabethans, who set many plays in Italy; Venice is the setting for *Othello*, as for Ben Jonson's play *Volpone* (1606). Shakespeare need not have visited Venice to know about gondolas, the Rialto, and the Duke or Doge for she had long been known to English travellers as the port to the East; Venice transported Crusaders, and transported and insured pilgrims to Jerusalem. Unlike England, Venice was not a nation ruled by a king but an ancient civic republic, commercially hospitable to foreigners from east, west and north, Greek, Jew or Protestant. Physically remarkable, built on a set of islands, a unique, dignified, artistic, luxurious and splendid city, she was Catholic but politically independent. Like England, she was insular and dependent on sea-borne trade. Venice's credit was good by reason of her reputation for strictly enforcing her laws, even against her citizens. The word of a merchant of Venice was his bond. Venice was at one end of the chain of mercantile cities in Europe, London at the other; both were centres of marine insurance and venture capital. Jews were tolerated in Venice, and lived in the original (walled) Ghetto, not mentioned by Shakespeare. The exoticism of Venice is seen at Belmont, a palatial estate of vague location. It can be reached by sailing, and also by the 'traject', the 'common ferry which trades to Venice'; the ferry point is twenty miles from Belmont, hence presumably on the Venetian mainland of Italy rather than on an island. The less exotic business of Venice is seen at its centre, on the Rialto. Shakespeare used all these ideas about Venice in his play, though he set it, consciously or not, in the days of its greatest prosperity around 1500.

**CHECK
THE BOOK**
The Oxford Companion to Shakespeare, ed. Michael Dobson and Stanley Wells, 2001, is a mine of historical and factual information about every aspect of Shakespeare, his works and his reputation.

World events	Shakespeare's life	Literature and the arts
1290 Jews expelled from England by Edward I		**Late 13th c** (*c.*) *Gesta Romanorum* (source)
1295 Marco Polo returns to Venice after travels in China		
1380 Venice's 100-year feud with Genoa ends		
1400–90 (*c.*) Venice at height of maritime power		
1492 Columbus sets sails for America		
1490s Venice's power at sea in decline		
1516 Jews in Venice confined to Ghetto		**1513** Niccolò Machiavelli, *The Prince*
		1528 Castiglione's *Book of the Courtier*
1534 Henry VIII breaks with Rome		
1556 Archbishop Cranmer burnt at stake		
1558 Elizabeth I accedes to throne		**1558** Trans. of Ser Giovanni of Florence, *Il Pecorone* (late 14th-c. source)
		1562 Lope de Vega, Spanish dramatist, born
	1564 (26 April) **William Shakespeare** baptised, Stratford-upon-Avon	

World events	Shakespeare's life	Literature and the arts
1566 Royal Exchange founded		
1570 Elizabeth I excommunicated by Pope Pius V		
1572 Death of Venetian painter Titian	**1576** James Burbage builds the first theatre in England, at Shoreditch	
1577 Francis Drake sets out on voyage round the world		
		1578 (*c.*) *The Jew* (lost play -? source)
		1580 (*c.*) Sir Philip Sidney, *An Apologie for Poetrie*; Anthony Munday, *Zelauto* (source)
	1582 Shakespeare marries Anne Hathaway	
	1583 Their daughter, Susanna, is born	
1584 Raleigh's sailors land in Virginia	**1585** Their twins, Hamnet and Judith, born	
1587 Execution of Mary Queen of Scots	**late 1580s – early 90s** Probably writes *Henry VI (Parts I, II, III)* and *Richard III*	**1588-9** Thomas Kyd, *The Spanish Tragedy*
1588 The Spanish Armada defeated		**1589** Christopher Marlowe, *The Jew of Malta* (source)

World events	Shakespeare's life	Literature and the arts
		1590 Edmund Spenser, *Faerie Queene* (Books I-III)
1592 Rialto Bridge completed. Plague in London closes theatres	**1592** Recorded as being a London actor and an 'upstart crow'	
	1592–4 Writes *Comedy of Errors*	
	1594 onwards Writes exclusively for the Lord Chamberlain's Men	
	1595 (pre-) *Two Gentlemen of Verona*, *The Taming of the Shrew* and *Love's Labour's Lost* probably written	
	1595 (c.) *Romeo and Juliet*	
1596 English raid on Cadiz	**1596-8** First performance, *The Merchant of Venice*	**1596** English trans. of Alexandre Silvain, *The Orator* (source)
	1598/9 Globe Theatre built at Southwark	
	1600 *A Midsummer Night's Dream*, *Much Ado about Nothing* and *The Merchant of Venice* printed in quartos	
	1600–1 *Hamlet*	
	1600–2 *Twelfth Night* written	

World events	Shakespeare's life	Literature and the arts
1603 Death of Queen Elizabeth Tudor; accession of James Stuart	**1603** onwards His company enjoys patronage of James I as the King's Men	
	1604 *Othello* performed	
1605 Discovery of Guy Fawkes's plot	**1605** First version of *King Lear*	**1605** Cervantes, *Don Quijote de la Mancha*
	1606 *Macbeth*	
	1606–7 *Antony and Cleopatra*	
	1608 The King's Men acquire Blackfriars Theatre for winter performances	
1610 William Harvey discovers circulation of blood		
	1611 *Cymbeline, The Winter's Tale* and *The Tempest* performed	
	1613 Globe Theatre burns down	
1618 Raleigh executed for treason Thirty Years War begins in Europe	**1616** Death of William Shakespeare	
		1622 Birth of French dramatist Moliére
1655 Under Cromwell. Jews formally readmitted to England	**1623** First Folio of Shakespeare's works	

EDITIONS OF *THE MERCHANT OF VENICE*

Below are the most common modern editions:

John Russell Brown, ed., The Arden Shakespeare, Methuen, 1955, revised 1961
  Good full academic edition, with reliable glosses and notes; though now a little old it is fuller than Mahood or Halio

J.L. Halio, ed., The Oxford Shakespeare, Clarendon Press, 1993; World Classics, Oxford University Press, 1994
  Excellent. Full academic edition, with reliable glosses and notes

G.B. Harrison, ed., Penguin Shakespeare, Penguin Popular Classics, 1955
  A school edition, originally published in the 1930s; in its Popular Classic form it has no introduction or notes and is not ideal for examinees

Bernard Lott, ed., New Swan Shakespeare, Longman, 1962, 1964
  A school edition with good notes, except on matters which might bring a blush to the cheek of the young person

M.M. Mahood, ed., New Cambridge Shakespeare, Cambridge University Press, 1987
  Mahood is a literary critic as well as a scholar. A good full academic edition. This is the text which has been used to accompany these Notes

W. Moelwyn Merchant, ed., The New Penguin Shakespeare, Penguin, 1967
  Better than Harrison. Some notes. Eccentric introduction

Kenneth Myrick, ed., The Signet Shakespeare, Signet, 1965
  A good college edition

J.H. Walter, ed., The Players' Shakespeare, Heinemann, 1960
  A school edition which silently omits text which might be considered *risqué*

SINGLE-VOLUME COLLECTED EDITIONS

Peter Alexander, ed., *William Shakespeare: the Complete Works*, Collins, 1951
  Convenient: good brief introductions, simple glossary, but no notes

Stanley Wells and Gary Taylor, gen. eds, *Works*, Oxford University Press, 1986 (known as the Oxford Shakespeare)
> The version sold as the Compact Edition of the Oxford Shakespeare is convenient, and has good introductions, simple glossary, but no notes. However, a radical editorial policy has changed familiar texts in ways that some scholars dislike or dispute. But the Oxford Shakespeare is already influential

CRITICAL WORKS

C. L. Barber, *Shakespeare's Festive Comedy*, 2nd edn, Oxford University Press, 1972
> A good general study of the comedies

J.C. Bulman, *Text in Performance: The Merchant of Venice*, Manchester University Press, 1991
> Theatre history

Michael Dobson and Stanley Wells, eds, *The Oxford Companion to Shakespeare*, OUP 2001.
> A mine of information

John Gross, *Shylock: Four Hundred Years in the Life of a Legend*, Vintage, 1994
> A wide-ranging survey

Toby Lelyveld, *Shylock on the Stage*, 1960 (Publisher unknown).
> Theatre history

John Lyon, *The Merchant of Venice*, Harvester, 1988
> A sophisticated introduction which pays attention to recent criticism

Murray Roston, *Sixteenth-Century English Literature*, Macmillan, 1982
> A sound general introduction, with a good sketch of Shakespeare's literary career

John Wilders, ed., *'The Merchant of Venice': A Casebook*, Macmillan, 1962
> A selection of critical articles

OTHER TITLES CITED IN THESE NOTES

W.H. Auden, *The Dyer's Hand and Other Essays,* Faber and Faber, 1963

Jonathan Bate, *The Genius of Shakespeare*, Picador, 1997

Cicely Berry, *The Actor and His Text*, Harrap, 1987

Philip Brockbank 'Shakespeare and the Fashion of These Times', *Shakespeare Survey*, vol.16, 1963

Deborah Cartmell, *Interpreting Shakespeare on Screen*, Macmillan, 2000

David Crystal, *Shakespeare's Words*, Penguin, 2002

Eamon Duffy, *The Stripping of the Altars*, New Haven, 1992

Park Honan, *Shakespeare: A Life*, Oxford University Press, 1998

S. S.Hussey, *The Literary Language of Shakespeare*, Longman, 1982

Andrew Gurr, *The Shakespearean Stage*, Cambridge University Press, 1992

Frank Kermode, *Shakespeare's Language*, Allen Lane, 2000

J. W. Lever, 'Shylock, Portia and the Values of Shakespearean Comedy ', *Shakespeare Quarterly*, vol. 3, 1952

Russ McDonald, *Shakespeare and the Arts of Language*, Oxford University Press, 2001

Diarmaid MacCulloch, *Reformation: Europe's House Divided 1490–1700*, Penguin, 2003

Michael Mangan, *A Preface to Shakespeare's Comedies*, Longman, 1996

Patsy Rodenburg, *Speaking Shakespeare*, Methuen, 2002

Carol Rumens, ed., *Clamorous Voices: Shakespeare's Women Today*, Women's Press, 1987

S. Schoenbaum *Shakespeare's Lives*, Oxford University Press, revised edn., 1991

Ann Thompson, *Shakespeare's Chaucer: A Study in Literary Origins*, Liverpool University Press, 1978

allegory the sustained suggestion of deeper, usually moral, meaning in a story

aside a stage direction indicating the convention that the following speech is supposed to be inaudible to other characters onstage; like a soliloquy, it serves to communicate private thoughts

comedic characteristic of comedy and of the conventions of comedy, when a confusion of identities is resolved in a happy ending; as distinct from comic, laughable

couplet a pair of rhyming lines

decorum rhetorical principle that style must match topic, and that there is a hierarchy of suitable styles: high for tragedy, low for farce, and so forth

exposition the giving of information essential to the story

irony saying one thing while meaning another; using words to convey the opposite of their literal meaning; saying something that has one meaning for someone knowledgeable about a situation and another meaning for those who are not; incongruity between what might be expected and what actually happens; ill-timed arrival of an event which had been hoped for

malapropism using the wrong word; from French *mal à propos*; after Mrs Malaprop (Mrs Mistake) in Sheridan's *The Rivals*, 1755

mock-heroic using heroic comparisons for playful purposes

paradox a statement that seems self-contradictory, absurd or unbelievable, yet which contains a truth

parody imitation of the style of a well-known work, exaggerating its features for comic purposes

register linguistic term for the level of the vocabulary from which words are taken, see decorum

romance a story of marvellous adventure, with elements of folk- and fairytale, in which wishes are fulfilled: the right casket is chosen; long-lost relatives are reunited; Jack shall have Jill and all shall be well. Often combined with comedy; not necessarily a love story, in the modern sense of the word 'romantic'

stage business physical actions accompanying or clarifying the words of the actors

Mary Alexander has a degree in English from the University of Melbourne and Diplomas in Education from La Trobe University and the Institute of Education, London University. She has taught English literature in schools in Australia and Britain.

Michael Alexander has recently retired from the Alexander Berry Chair of English Literature in the University of St Andrews. He has edited *The Canterbury Tales: The First Fragment* for Penguin, and *The Canterbury Tales: Illustrated Prologue* for Scala Books, and written a York Note on Chaucer's *Knight's Tale*. He has also translated *Beowulf* and other Old English poems into verse for Penguin Classics. His *History of English Literature* is published by Palgrave Macmillan.

General Editor
Martin Gray, former Head of the Department of English Studies at the University of Stirling, and of Literary Studies at the University of Luton.

Maya Angelou
I Know Why the Caged Bird Sings

Jane Austen
Pride and Prejudice

Alan Ayckbourn
Absent Friends

Elizabeth Barrett Browning
Selected Poems

Robert Bolt
A Man for All Seasons

Harold Brighouse
Hobson's Choice

Charlotte Brontë
Jane Eyre

Emily Brontë
Wuthering Heights

Shelagh Delaney
A Taste of Honey

Charles Dickens
David Copperfield
Great Expectations
Hard Times
Oliver Twist

Roddy Doyle
Paddy Clarke Ha Ha Ha

George Eliot
Silas Marner
The Mill on the Floss

Anne Frank
The Diary of a Young Girl

William Golding
Lord of the Flies

Oliver Goldsmith
She Stoops to Conquer

Willis Hall
The Long and the Short and the Tall

Thomas Hardy
Far from the Madding Crowd
The Mayor of Casterbridge
Tess of the d'Urbervilles
The Withered Arm and other Wessex Tales

L.P. Hartley
The Go-Between

Seamus Heaney
Selected Poems

Susan Hill
I'm the King of the Castle

Barry Hines
A Kestrel for a Knave

Louise Lawrence
Children of the Dust

Harper Lee
To Kill a Mockingbird

Laurie Lee
Cider with Rosie

Arthur Miller
The Crucible
A View from the Bridge

Robert O'Brien
Z for Zachariah

Frank O'Connor
My Oedipus Complex and Other Stories

George Orwell
Animal Farm

J.B. Priestley
An Inspector Calls
When We Are Married

Willy Russell
Educating Rita
Our Day Out

J.D. Salinger
The Catcher in the Rye

William Shakespeare
Henry IV Part I
Henry V
Julius Caesar
Macbeth
The Merchant of Venice
A Midsummer Night's Dream
Much Ado About Nothing
Romeo and Juliet
The Tempest
Twelfth Night

George Bernard Shaw
Pygmalion

Mary Shelley
Frankenstein

R.C. Sherriff
Journey's End

Rukshana Smith
Salt on the snow

John Steinbeck
Of Mice and Men

Robert Louis Stevenson
Dr Jekyll and Mr Hyde

Jonathan Swift
Gulliver's Travels

Robert Swindells
Daz 4 Zoe

Mildred D. Taylor
Roll of Thunder, Hear My Cry

Mark Twain
Huckleberry Finn

James Watson
Talking in Whispers

Edith Wharton
Ethan Frome

William Wordsworth
Selected Poems

A Choice of Poets

Mystery Stories of the Nineteenth Century including The Signalman

Nineteenth Century Short Stories

Poetry of the First World War

Six Women Poets

For the AQA Anthology:

Duffy and Armitage & Pre-1914 Poetry

Heaney and Clarke & Pre-1914 Poetry

Poems from Different Cultures

Margaret Atwood
Cat's Eye
The Handmaid's Tale

Jane Austen
Emma
Mansfield Park
Persuasion
Pride and Prejudice
Sense and Sensibility

Alan Bennett
Talking Heads

William Blake
Songs of Innocence and of Experience

Charlotte Brontë
Jane Eyre
Villette

Emily Brontë
Wuthering Heights

Angela Carter
Nights at the Circus

Geoffrey Chaucer
The Franklin's Prologue and Tale
The Merchant's Prologue and Tale
The Miller's Prologue and Tale
The Prologue to the Canterbury Tales
The Wife of Bath's Prologue and Tale

Samuel Coleridge
Selected Poems

Joseph Conrad
Heart of Darkness

Daniel Defoe
Moll Flanders

Charles Dickens
Bleak House
Great Expectations
Hard Times

Emily Dickinson
Selected Poems

John Donne
Selected Poems

Carol Ann Duffy
Selected Poems

George Eliot
Middlemarch
The Mill on the Floss

T.S. Eliot
Selected Poems
The Waste Land

F. Scott Fitzgerald
The Great Gatsby

E.M. Forster
A Passage to India

Brian Friel
Translations

Thomas Hardy
Jude the Obscure
The Mayor of Casterbridge
The Return of the Native
Selected Poems
Tess of the d'Urbervilles

Seamus Heaney
Selected Poems from 'Opened Ground'

Nathaniel Hawthorne
The Scarlet Letter

Homer
The Iliad
The Odyssey

Aldous Huxley
Brave New World

Kazuo Ishiguro
The Remains of the Day

Ben Jonson
The Alchemist

James Joyce
Dubliners

John Keats
Selected Poems

Philip Larkin
The Whitsun Weddings and Selected Poems

Christopher Marlowe
Doctor Faustus
Edward II

Arthur Miller
Death of a Salesman

John Milton
Paradise Lost Books I & II

Toni Morrison
Beloved

George Orwell
Nineteen Eighty-Four

Sylvia Plath
Selected Poems

Alexander Pope
Rape of the Lock & Selected Poems

William Shakespeare
Antony and Cleopatra
As You Like It
Hamlet
Henry IV Part I
King Lear
Macbeth
Measure for Measure
The Merchant of Venice
A Midsummer Night's Dream
Much Ado About Nothing
Othello
Richard II
Richard III
Romeo and Juliet
The Taming of the Shrew
The Tempest
Twelfth Night
The Winter's Tale

George Bernard Shaw
Saint Joan

Mary Shelley
Frankenstein

Jonathan Swift
Gulliver's Travels and A Modest Proposal

Alfred Tennyson
Selected Poems

Virgil
The Aeneid

Alice Walker
The Color Purple

Oscar Wilde
The Importance of Being Earnest

Tennessee Williams
A Streetcar Named Desire
The Glass Menagerie

Jeanette Winterson
Oranges Are Not the Only Fruit

John Webster
The Duchess of Malfi

Virginia Woolf
To the Lighthouse

William Wordsworth
The Prelude and Selected Poems

W.B. Yeats
Selected Poems

Metaphysical Poets